GOD
CAN DO IT-
Without Me!

GOD
CAN DO IT-
Without Me!

JOHANNES FACIUS

SOVEREIGN WORLD BOOKS

Sovereign World Ltd
PO Box 777
Tonbridge
Kent TN11 0ZS

ISBN 1-85240-054-4

Printed in England by Clays Ltd, St Ives plc.

Contents

Foreword

I have known Johannes Facius closely for over thirty years and am a witness to the testimony which he has given in these pages. Although it is a special joy for me to write this foreword, it does not really need an introduction. It is a highly moving account of a man truly born of God, with a genuine experience of the Holy Spirit, totally committed to the Lord Jesus and His service, who nevertheless is led into a fiery trial of his faith. Under no circumstances would I have ever described Johannes as 'superficial'. Yet it seemed as if Satan himself had him in his grip, torturing him and accusing him.

At times it appeared to some of us as if nothing was left—no faith, no joy, no power or authority, very little life and certainly no peace! But from the moment this servant of God's trial began, I knew by the Spirit that the Lord was leading him along a special path, which few could tread and few could understand. And in the end Johannes came out with a testimony to the grace and faithfulness of God, and a heart knowledge of the Lord which nothing in this universe will ever be able to take away.

From his story I believe we can learn three vital lessons.

Firstly: the Lord only tests what He knows can be proven to be of Himself in us. If there is any chance of His work in us being destroyed, He will not test it. It is the proving of our faith that it may be found unto praise and glory and honour at the revelation of Jesus Christ (1 Peter 1:7). In the trial what is worthless is destroyed, and what is eternal is purified and preserved.

Secondly: when the Lord is preparing vessels chosen for specific tasks either in time or in eternity or for both, He puts that vessel through unusual and especial processes. In the end it is eternal character for which the Lord is seeking.

Thirdly: sometimes the Lord makes one of His servants a 'prophetic sign' to His people. I believe that Johannes has been made such a sign. Unless we learn by the Spirit to dig deep and build our lives on the solid rock of the person and work of the Lord Jesus, we will never be able to stand during the shaking and storms of the last era of world history. Times of enormous and demonic testing and trial are coming on the face of the earth. Our self-manufactured Christianity, our secondhand head knowledge of the Lord will break down at that point, as will the kind of faith which is not anchored in God Himself but in subjective emotions, in the outward trappings of Christian work and witness, in the high powered atmosphere of large meetings. We need to take heed and allow the Lord to deal with us now and thus prepare us for the responsibilities and tasks that lie ahead. The Lord is not interested in our destruction or failure but in our preservation and overcoming. To that end He will use even Satan to divide the chaff in us from the wheat. His goal is that our spirit and soul and body may be preserved entire without blame at the coming of our Lord Jesus Christ (1 Thessalonians 5:23).

Lance Lambert

Chapter 1

SHOT DOWN IN MOSCOW

IT ALL BEGAN in Moscow. Or should I rather say, it all culminated in Moscow. Together with other international prayer leaders, I had taken a team of intercessors from different countries into the capital city of the Soviet Union. Our assignment was to do spiritual warfare against the 'spiritual Pharaoh', who was preventing the Soviet Jews from returning to the Promised Land. This prayer action was the outcome of several prayer conferences in Israel and elsewhere dealing with the vital issue of Soviet Jewry being held captive by the communist authorities. We had felt for a long time that the real hindrance was not an earthly atheistic power, but one of the strongest demonic forces of all times: that of anti-Semitism.

The time of our visit to Moscow was over New Year 1985/86, long before the breakdown of communist power. Mr Gorbachev had been in power only a few months, and there were not yet any major changes through *perestroika* or *glasnost*. We were still suffering under the old dark cloud of Leninism. Little did any of us in the team think that just a year later another revolution would take place and change the map of central Europe. As we made our Jericho march around the Kremlin Wall, praying for the downfall of the evil power keeping the Jews in bondage, we could not have imagined that a couple of years later Jewish people would leave the Soviet Union and return to Israel in such great numbers that the nation of Israel could hardly cope with them. The Lord certainly answered prayers beyond what we could ask or even think. I am not taking the credit for this on behalf of our little team. But we do know that hundreds of thousands of God's children have been praying for this over the last forty years. We also know that over the years many other prayer teams went into Moscow and prayed on location for the downfall of communism. We were just one of many such teams.

Even today, after it has all happened, it is still hard to believe. Many of us were like those in the early church who prayed for the apostle Peter, in prison in Jerusalem. When the angel released him from prison and he went to meet his friends in the house where 'many people...were praying' for him, they could not believe that it really was him, but thought it was his ghost. How much unbelief there is even among us intercessors!

The assignment we were on in Moscow included several types of prayer and spiritual warfare. Among other things we were to walk to the head office of the Central Committee of the Communist Party, where Mr Gorbachev had his office, just to let him know in spirit that he was not the new ruler over the Soviet Union. That position belonged to the Lord Jesus Christ, and unless he (Mr Gorbachev) would fall in line with God's purposes for both the Soviet Jews, the Christians and also the Russian people, whom God loves, he would soon be out of business.

Another action, the one I considered the most important, was to go through the Lenin Mausoleum and pronounce a judgement upon the 'god of the Soviet system'—an idol by the name of Vladimir Lenin, the founder of the communist state. The Soviet system has always claimed to be non-religious, to be a purely atheistic society, but how wrong they have been in this. On my travels in the Soviet Union I have easily been able to discern that the Soviet system has been one of the most religious systems that ever existed. The Soviets did not worship our God and Father, the Creator of the universe, but they worshipped their own god and father—Lenin! All over the Soviet Union you find giant statues of Lenin. Once a year every school class has to go to a statue of Lenin to pay their respects, to worship the father of the nation. Besides that, you find in every town gigantic memorials to the heroic Red Army and their victorious fight in 'the great patriotic war' (World War II). When you combine this with the fact that millions pass by the remains of the dead Lenin every year as he lies in the Lenin Mausoleum in Red Square, you come to the conclusion that the Soviets are worshipping a spirit of death.

Before we went to the Lenin Mausoleum we sought the Lord in prayer in order to know what He wanted us to do. There was no way, of course, in which we could conduct an ordinary prayer meeting inside. You are not even allowed to stop inside, but must follow the long line of people, and the whole mausoleum is packed with guards who watch over you like a hawk over its prey. We knew we had only a few minutes and so it was important to make use of the time to express something which could resist and damage this spirit of death.

During the time of prayer I received a word which became our ammunition against the Enemy. Jesus spoke these words to the barren fig tree: 'May you never bear fruit again' (Mt 21:19). And the tree withered and died at these powerful words. We understood from this that we were all to repeat a proclamation as we walked through the mausoleum: 'You spirit of death! We curse you in the name of the Lord Jesus. No one shall never again eat fruit from you!' It was not possible to speak the words out loud, but we were all to whisper them together, over and over again, until we came out at the other end of Lenin's tomb.

Counter-attack

I believe that we did the right thing, and that we received this from the Lord. I also believe that I probably did not fully realize what we in fact were doing: taking on one of the most powerful demonic forces in the world, unaware that such an attack on the gates of hell would provoke the powers of darkness to strike back.

11

It was through this move against the Enemy that I suffered one of the most strange attacks of sickness that I have ever experienced. When I woke up the next morning I felt that all my strength had left me. I was so weak that I could not get out of bed. A strange spirit of utter weakness and discomfort had apparently hit me. I lost my appetite, got a fever and felt my whole body was paralyzed. At that time I did not think about it in terms other than having caught the flu or some similar ailment, but later on I began to understand that something of that spirit of death, which we had resisted in the Lenin Mausoleum, had somehow been able to make a counter-attack on me. When it was discovered three months later that I had developed a heart disease, the first thing the doctors asked me was this: 'Did you at any time over the last months or weeks suffer any kind of virus attack?' Since they could not find any kind of physical cause for this disturbance in the heart rhythm, they told me that this kind of sickness is sometimes triggered by the flu or a virus. I know that what hit me in Moscow looked like a virus, but that it wasn't. It was a demonic counter-attack. The strange thing is that although I have never before or since felt so sick in all of my life, the illness lasted only one day, no doubt due to the powerful intercession of my brothers in the team. We had already organized a prayer chain, taking turns around the clock, realizing that we needed all the protection we could get because of the nature of our mission. Now the brothers intensified their prayers for me. Towards midnight that same day, when we were planning to have a special celebration of the Lord's Supper on the bank of the River Moskva, I was back on my feet again. Some of the brothers told me that they had never seen anyone who had been so ill recover so quickly. Today I realize one thing about sicknesses caused by demonic attacks: they leave as quickly as they come! This is another proof that I was under demonic influence. Later on, when after almost three years of severe depression I was delivered, the deliverance took place in less than thirty seconds.

Know your Enemy

Through this strange experience and through what happened afterwards I have learned some important things concerning spiritual warfare.

It is wise and commendable never to underestimate our Enemy. Today we encounter Christians and even ministers of God's word who seem to fall into the trap of ridiculing the devil. They somehow think that the finished work of the Lord Jesus, who completely vanquished Satan on the cross, gives us the liberty to kick the Enemy around as we see fit. This is a dangerous misconception, and besides, it is totally against Scripture! Did not the apostle Jude warn us against this? In his Epistle he clearly warns us against reviling high principalities and powers (vv. 8–9). He reminds us about the archangel Michael who disputed with the devil about the body of Moses, and did not dare to pronounce any railing judgement against him, but said, 'The Lord rebuke you!' How can we think for a moment that we are more powerful than the archangel Michael? How much foolishness there is in the body of Christ concerning this matter!

Some time ago, when I was visiting the States, I turned on the television one Sunday morning to watch one of the many Christian programmes. A fairly well known tele-evangelist was trying to teach his congregation how to handle the devil. In so doing he pretended to be a dog trainer, treating the devil as a dog and ordering him around by the usual commands. As I watched this appalling show of childish and foolish behaviour I said to my wife, 'If this brother does not repent of his folly, he will be in trouble pretty soon.' I later learned that this man did repent and changed his attitude. Praise the Lord!

When I was a soldier I learned that a good soldier is one who never underestimates his enemy, but always has great respect for his opponent. The soldier who brags about never being fearful of anything or anybody eventually gets not only himself killed, but also brings the whole army into danger. The present-day claim that the victory of the Lord Jesus, applied to our situation in the world, is to be understood as a *carte blanche* to have a go at the Enemy at any time is immature and premature, not in accordance with either the word of God or the realities of this life. It leads to illusions which in turn could lead to spiritual deception, and it causes much suffering and pain among those who are not sufficiently rooted in Christ.

Some may justify themselves by saying, 'Well, I didn't want you to suffer any physical attacks due to spiritual warfare!' Maybe not, but the Enemy has other means. If you are not careful, you might find that you could be deceived into some kind of isolation, overemphasis or plain error, or you might without knowing it become proud of your achievements. The Enemy is very subtle and has more than one way of trapping us. It is healthy to be a little fearful. I am not talking about a fear which paralyzes us in our battle against the Enemy. I am talking only about caution that makes us watchful.

What would your reaction be if a big African lion entered your church while you were sitting there? I am sure that no one would go to sleep that day. We believers have developed a habit of sleeping in the presence of the Lord sometimes, but if we realized that the devil is also present among us, going around like a roaring lion seeking whom to devour, we would not find it easy to fall asleep any more.

Some years ago I visited the beautiful Kruger National Park in South Africa. As we drove along in the car we suddenly discovered some lion cubs playing in the ditch. Wanting to get some good shots with my camera of these sweet little lions, I grabbed hold of the doorhandle, ready to get out. But my friend quickly grabbed my arm and pulled me back. He warned me that any approach to the lion cubs would immediately provoke the appearance of the mother, who was just behind the trees. My foolishness could make me end up as lions' food and endanger every-one. I was safe only inside the Range Rover. We are also safe only as we learn to abide in Christ and never become so overconfident in ourselves that we leave Him in order to encounter the Enemy on our own.

Another thing we need to understand is this: if we attack the powers of darkness, they will strike back at us. This should not prevent us in any way from progressing in the war, but it should perhaps tell us that, as in any war, there is the possibility of being hit and wounded. There can be no war without casualties. Our job is to consider the risk and do whatever we can to minimize the loss. In this respect I admire the attitude of the Israeli army: their high regard for human life has helped them to conduct warfare in such a way that has lessened the loss of their men. However, there is a price to be paid if we want to be engaged in the battle for the kingdom. If we think we will never be hurt, shot at, bothered or harassed by anybody we are not fit for the army of the Lord. We will only end up utterly frustrated and disappointed.

I have never regretted joining the army of the Lord. I am not going to quit, even after having gone through three years of pain that nearly cost me my life and the life of my dear family. My reason for writing this book is not to discourage anybody from participating in the battle, because I believe we are called to that battle, but rather to share my experiences in order to make us all better soldiers, fighting in the right way, according to the biblical rules and with the spiritual weapons. I have no illusions about the possibilities of getting into trouble. I do not agree with those who teach that because we are born again we are totally safe and immune to the wiles of the devil, and consequently we can do whatever we like with him without expecting trouble. There is a price to be paid, partly because of our mistakes in the war, and partly just because we are in the battle and are being exposed to the powers of darkness. Let us decide that we are soldiers, and every soldier is prepared to suffer and eventually, if need be, to lose his life.

Protective covering

Why was I shot down in Moscow? There can only be one answer: I was not covered the way I should have been. I could also say that I was not sufficiently aware of the importance of covering at that time, and therefore I had to be taught some vital lessons.

There are basically three aspects of this matter of covering that we need to pay attention to. First, what I would call the overall covering: abiding in Christ! Safety is of the Lord, and it is not enough to be taught certain procedures from the Bible. We need to understand what it means to stay close to the Lord, to abide in Christ. To explain that is quite simple.

Jesus said that if we abide in Him and His words in us, we can ask anything we wish, and it will be given to us (Jn 15:7). This simply means we are to stay in unbroken intimate fellowship with the Lord, to hear His voice, receive and obey His word, and communicate with Him in prayer. If this precious, unceasing communion with the Lord is in any way broken off, we lose our covering.

This is what happened to me. Due to too much busyness—busyness in the Lord's business—I came to the point where I began to let go of my dependency on the Lord in the word and in prayer. After many years of experience in this whole area of prayer and intercession, I began to go by my great routine. The gift and the anointing were there, so I slipped away from the 'fear and trembling' attitude which keeps us aware of our own weakness and need for the Lord's daily mercy. Did not the Lord say to His disciples in the Garden of Gethsemane, 'Watch and pray so that you will not fall into temptation. The spirit is willing, but the body is weak' (Mt. 26:41)?

We will never be so clever, so experienced and spiritually mature that we no longer need to stay close to the Lord. On the contrary, if things are developing as they should in our lives, we will become more and more dependent on the Lord the longer we live and the more we come to know Him. Those who try to tell us that we who have received the power of the Spirit and His anointing no longer have any need to ask, to pray or to inquire of the Lord, have gone terribly wrong and are doing much harm not only to themselves, but to the whole body of the Lord's people. Because I became sloppy in this area, the flesh became susceptible to the Enemy's attack.

When I was a young Christian I learned that we have to discern between spirit and flesh, and that the only way to do that is through intimate communion with the Lord. I was also told that we need to fear the works of the flesh, because the flesh is in coalition with the Enemy of our souls, and opening up to the flesh is the same as opening up to the powers of darkness.

I am well aware of the danger of overemphasizing this. Every kind of fear can start to paralyze us. We can become so afraid of the flesh that we do not dare to move. This is not the intention. On the other hand, we cannot overlook the ever present possibility of the influence of the flesh, and must remember that only by continual walking in the Spirit can we put the works of the flesh to death. Today we have moved away from this truth, and this is one of the reasons why we in the charismatic movement are in a mess. We must give ourselves to the word and prayer as never before, and we must teach the body to be utterly dependent on the Lord in everything we do, otherwise we give room for the flesh, and the flesh will lead us astray, not only the bad aspects of the flesh, but also the good works of the flesh. Everything we do outside of an intimate, dependent communion with the Lord is flesh and will never become anything else but flesh. Personal 'watching and praying' can never be substituted by any charismatic gift or anointing.

Another aspect of covering is to walk in the light, giving no ground for thoughts or actions not pleasing to the Lord. We are covered by the blood of Jesus, the Lamb of God, as long as we deal with everything that creeps into our minds. We do not have to perform any particular ceremony or repeat a formula for the blood of the Lamb to cover us. We only have to make sure that we have confessed our sins properly and received His forgiveness by faith. Christians all over the world are mistaken concerning the power of the blood, and some believe that for the blood to cover us we need to follow certain procedures. May I suggest that instead of all this—much of which comes close to magic and occult practices—we simply learn the good old way: to humble ourselves before God and men and learn to confess our sins and receive forgiveness? If I had kept my heart and mind clean from anything displeasing to the Lord, the Enemy would not have been able to find a foothold in my soul and drag me down into depression and suffering.

Still this is not enough. Others, too, need to cover us. Paul writes to his brothers and sisters in Rome:

> I urge you, brothers, by our Lord Jesus Christ and by the love of the Spirit, to join me in my struggle by praying to God for me. Pray that I may be rescued from the unbelievers in Judea and that my service in Jerusalem may be acceptable to the saints there (Rom 15:30–31).

Paul was a beggar. He did not beg for anyone's money— we could learn much from that today—but for the covering of prayers from his fellow believers. I have to admit that I have never been good at begging for money. I do not feel that this is something I have the freedom in the Lord to do. Some have told me that this attitude of mine is the reason for my ministry not really developing into the 'worldwide' type. Well, I do not care about that, and by the way I do not think it is honouring to the Lord to beg for material things. To me this represents a real lack of faith, and I am amazed to find that those who claim to have the most faith are often those who beg the most. If they really had the big faith they claim, why cannot they trust God for their needs? I just fail to see the 'light' here. Oh, how much unreality there is in the Christian world today!

However, I would like to become a beggar in another area: begging for the prayers of the saints that I might be delivered from all the schemes of the Enemy! This is an area where I failed myself and my family. Again, I probably felt that it was not necessary, or maybe that the prayers of the saints should be used for other more important matters. We believers are often either too proud or too humble.

One of the reasons for deciding to publish a regular newsletter after my healing and restoration was to remedy my lack of prayer covering. We need one another's prayers in the body these days, and we need to mobilize prayer partners for every single action we undertake in the future. I have come to see that I am no good on my own. I am no match for the Enemy on my own. I need to be linked with the body and to be covered by its love and support. I do not believe those who tell us that every individual believer in himself has ever present and unlimited power and authority over the Evil One and can kick the devil around as he sees fit. This is not true. This is not the word of God. My personal testimony is that such an independent reliance on one's own position is asking for serious trouble. We need the covering of the brethren, and, as for myself, I have joined the group of spiritual prayer beggars in the body of Christ.

Chapter 2

THROUGH THE FIRE

HAVE YOU EVER noticed how much the spiritual atmosphere in nations today can differ? When you travel much as I have been doing, you are often amazed at the changes of atmosphere you experience when you cross national borders. Shortly after the visit to Moscow I went with my wife to South Africa, at a time when racial tension was at its very peak, and that could certainly be felt. To me it is an ever growing conviction that the spirit of a nation is dominated not by political, social, cultural or even racial issues, but by unseen powers of darkness who do their utmost to destroy human lives. No wonder the apostle Paul underlines the fact that 'our struggle is not against flesh and blood, but against the rulers, against the authorities, against the powers of this dark world and against the spiritual forces of evil in the heavenly realms' (Eph 6:12).

Years ago when I used to visit Germany (where I have since settled with my wife) I often felt pressurized and downcast by a strange atmosphere of oppression due to the past dark history of that nation. But not so any more. Actually today I find it more easy to live in Germany than in my native country, Denmark, where the moral climate has been deteriorating year after year. The reason for the change in Germany is quite obvious to me. Large numbers of German Christians have dealt with their past history as intercessors. The whole question of the Holocaust has been repented of again and again over many years, perhaps almost too often. But God has honoured this move of His people, and today it is my experience that Germany is one of the brightest spiritual nations in the world.

'Be still'

As we ministered in South Africa I felt a much heavier oppression than on any of my previous trips. In part this was also due to a factor which led to my final breakdown: I was exhausted and becoming 'burned out', a syndrome which has hit so many of the Lord's servants in recent years. At that time I was 'only' holding seven spiritual leadership responsibilities. Although some of these responsibilities did not require much actual work, the very sense of being responsible could weigh me down much more than several days of work; when something went wrong I felt very tense and even guilty. I should have told myself that this would not work out in the end, or better, I should have listened to the voice of the Lord. But the sad fact was that I was no longer within hearing range of the Holy Spirit. I had become so busy for the Lord that I had no time to be with the Lord any more. When someone who is supposed to be leading a worldwide prayer movement has no time himself to pray then something is terribly wrong. I remember that the Lord would try to get in touch with me and I would mentally take my diary, look up and suggest that we could get together, the Lord and I, in about three months' time!

There are many things and many sins that can wreck our lives as God's servants, but maybe the worst of them all is busyness. Did not the Lord warn against this specific danger in the last days, before the return of the Son of Man?

> Be careful, or your hearts will be weighed down with dissipation, drunkenness and the anxieties of life, and that day will close on you unexpectedly like a trap (Lk 21:34).

We think we have the right to be busy and simply apologize

for not doing the most important thing of all—being still and seeking God. Activity is not only one of the most ensnaring temptations, it is also very often a sign of sheer unbelief. So many pastors, ordinary Christians and churches function with ongoing, never ceasing activity which, if taken away, would cause the total collapse of that ministry or of that church. We have become afraid of just stopping and waiting on the Lord, lest we lose our pace or miss money in the collection box.

It is not my intention to deal with this problem in depth in this chapter, but just to underline that a major reason for my breakdown was the fact that I could no longer rest in the Lord for what I was called to do, neither could I leave in His hands that which I was not supposed to do. The government which is supposed to be on His shoulders was resting heavily on my own, even for things for which I knew only God could undertake. Such a development is often caused by a mixture of distrust in God and personal pride—a belief that only I can really do this.

Sometimes the spirit of pride can be very difficult to detect because it is mixed up with a sincere desire to carry out one's duties and not be negligent in any way. I did not in any conscious way think that I was somebody. I only felt that it was absolutely important, even crucial, that I was there to do whatever was needed in certain areas. I was the only one who could do these things—at least that was what I thought, and quite a number of people agreed with that. Little did I know that God can easily do without me but that in His mercy and grace He does not want to do without me. No one, least of all myself, is indispensable to God. Were that so, this world would be in a total mess, and there would be no hope for the future.

I personally feel, brothers and sisters, that in this charismatic age, we suffer from too much self-reliance. Maybe the discovery of the gifts of the Spirit, His power and anointing made us realize that we actually had something and could do some quite extraordinary things, and thus along the road we began to cling to our own potential and abilities. Even today, after this theology has proved to be totally fallacious, I hear preachers try to boost people's self-confidence, and even if it is called 'spiritual self-confidence' it is completely off the track. We do not need self-confidence, we need Christ-confidence. We need to be reassured of the power and all-sufficiency of the finished work of our Lord Jesus, and to become increasingly aware of our own weakness and inability, otherwise pride will creep in and ruin our lives and ministries however mighty and glorious they may seem, just as has already happened and is happening around the world today.

Jerusalem '86

Exhausted and under pressure, I left South Africa to go on to a major prophetic conference scheduled to be held at Mount Carmel and in Jerusalem. And if there had been spiritual oppression in South Africa, arriving in Israel was like going from the fire into the ashes. Many years of frequent ministry in Israel have convinced me of this: in no other place on earth is there such a concentration of spiritual powers of darkness!

The very fact that we had invited people with prophetic ministries to this gathering in order to focus on 'What God is saying to His people today' increased that pressure. If you know anything about prophetic people, you know that they are independent and stubborn because of the strong convictions they naturally possess due to their prophetic calling. To try to handle 150 prophets from all over the world is an impossible job, humanly speaking! We were exactly 153, as Peter van Woerden, a dear friend of mine, pointed out when he compared us with the 153 large fish Peter the apostle caught in his net by the power of the Master, Jesus. And so we were quite a mixture of prophetic people, but all able to say, 'Thus says the Lord!'

A year ahead of this conference I had been asked to join the leadership group, and so I took an extra burden upon myself. But let me make one thing very clear: my involvement with this conference and all the turmoil it brought with it, including the interpersonal fighting and disagreements in the leadership group, did not cause my sickness and the following mental breakdown! It was only one of the difficulties and battles that had been going on for several years.

As I share things from this gathering I can truly say that I have no bitterness in my soul against anybody, and that today I am actually very thankful for what I went through together with my brothers and sisters. Overall, my mention of this event only serves the purpose of throwing light upon my own situation and revealing my own folly and weaknesses in order to give more glory to the name of the Lord for whatever He did in my life and in the lives of so many of God's dear people. However, it must be clear to everyone that coming to such an important event with a worn out body and soul is asking for serious trouble. Added to this was the fact that the preparation work in the leadership group had suffered, for more than a year, from such disagreements and division that if I had still been hearing God's voice, I would have left the group long before we even started the actual conference. I was warned to do so by several, but because of my personal pride, mixed with a sense of loyalty, I did not pay attention to these warnings.

It does not take much to understand that holding such a major event—an international prophetic gathering—without absolute unity and love in the organizing leadership is to invite the Enemy to have a go at the whole thing. The very project, including the possibility of a united leadership, was in itself a major challenge to the powers of darkness and would have led to much resistance by the Enemy, but at least that would not have given the devil access to our hearts. But to challenge the powers of evil with a divided leadership group who distrusted one another was to open the door wide for the powers of evil to walk right into our midst. We did not realize that pride affected not only individuals, but the group as a whole. How on earth could we, as mature leaders, have imagined that it would be possible to hold such an event in that condition without wounding many people?

This is not to say that these gatherings in the spring of 1986 on Carmel and in Jerusalem were a total waste of time. On the contrary, they may prove in the light of eternity to be among the most profitable. For a start, it is important to mention that many of the people participating felt a great blessing, mainly, I believe, because of the Lord's overruling grace. Secondly, the so-called 'success' of a spiritual event in God's eyes looks quite different to what we human beings understand as a success. We seek to produce 'results' as proof of having succeeded in our ministry, but God is not interested in good numbers, streamlined messages or a strong, professional leadership. God is after spiritual things. He is more interested in forming and shaping the character of those involved, even if the overall event looks and feels like one big failure.

Actually, some of the failures in our lives have proved more 'successful' for God's purposes than most of our great 'victories'. Peter's large catch of 153 large fish resulted from his own initial failure. At first he set out in his own strength, toiled the whole night and caught nothing. Yielding then to the Lord's calling and word he found great success, through which he was deeply humbled and brought down to the feet of the Master. A failure was the experience which brought Peter into his spiritual ministry of fishing men for Christ.

When I look back on this gathering in Jerusalem, and this is in no way an overall analysis of the conference, only some of the messages were relevant to my personal situation. One prophetic message touched my heart in a special way and revealed to me God's purpose in calling us all together. It came through David Noakes from England. The Lord said:

> I have called you to go into the throne room of the
> universe, the place where I, who am high and holy, living
> eternally, have my throne, from which I will give you my
> counsel and my instructions.

26

There are many who call themselves my ambassadors, but who never come into my throne room to receive anointing and to hear the message I want them to carry out. Thus they go out to utter words that are not my words, and are without the anointing of my Holy Spirit. But to you I say: Commit yourselves afresh to me on this day and decide in your hearts to concentrate to enter into my presence to stay there and not go out, until I shall send you. Neither shall you utter anything with your lips in my name which you have not heard from me and from the holy place in my throne room.

My presence is a place of peace, light and truth; no disorder or confusion or darkness or lies can exist before my throne. I have not brought you to this place in order to give you any special message to deliver, but I have brought you here in order to equip you to be heralds of every message that I shall entrust unto you in the days to come. I have brought you here to cleanse your hearts in the water of repentance, and to cleanse your lips with a coal from the altar, so that you might be holy and speak my word to a people that are perishing because of lack of true vision.

Commit yourselves afresh to me. Depart from all double-mindedness and go forth as those who find their greatest pleasure in being before my throne both in times when I am speaking, and in times when I am silent. Depart from all worldliness, which defiles your lives, and move instead into the dwelling place of your God. Be like those who never before knew the blessing of being doorkeepers in my house and abandoning the tabernacle of evil. In this way you shall hear the pulse beat from my heart, and you shall be able to move beyond the place of seeing my works into the valuable satisfaction of understanding my ways. For in that position of consecration and holiness I will share my thoughts with those whom I am calling my friends and who love me so much, that they will come close to me and dwell where I am dwelling. When you have come so far that the greatest desire of your heart is to dwell in this place, you shall not have any difficulty in understanding what I am saying because all other voices will then be quenched. I will make you into a living message with the word of life flowing out of your heart and from your lips in the very same way as in the days of my flesh. Commune with the Father as I did and I will make you to be what I was then: Jesus in the world!

To me it is an amazing thought that God could call so many people together at such great expense in order primarily to draw them into His own presence, and not, as we would have expected, to have us speak out great messages to the world.

I often wonder how God can afford to do what He does with His people. For instance, to let one of this century's greatest and most gifted Bible teachers, Watchman Nee from China, be locked up in a communist prison for more than twenty years, allowing him to use his great gifts to translate communist rubbish into English. And yet during such a time of seemingly utter waste, the word of God spread around the world through the publication of books dealing with almost everything he shared from God's word! As we went through the fire, as someone put it, during the Carmel and Jerusalem gathering, God worked deeply in many of our lives. The gathering might have appeared to be a failure, but it is very possible that this time produced more fruit in our hearts and lives than many far more 'successful' conferences in which we participated.

What I saw as our greatest spiritual experience on Mount Carmel came out of a letter that was sent to the conference by a dear sister in Jerusalem. Somehow, without herself being able to participate in our Carmel gathering, she had felt in the Spirit that we were in trouble concerning understanding the direction God wanted us to take. In her letter she revealed how during prayer she received a most unusual thought from the Lord—that all of us gathered on Carmel should enter into a fast from words. The Bible verses she gave us were Ecclesiastes 5:1–3:

> Guard your steps when you go to the house of God. Go
> near to listen rather than to offer the sacrifice of fools, who
> do not know that they do wrong. Do not be quick with
> your mouth, do not be hasty in your heart to utter
> anything before God. God is in heaven and you are on
> earth, so let your words be few. As a dream comes when
> there are many cares, so the speech of a fool when there
> are many words.

It is impossible really to express how powerfully these words hit us in the leadership in the midst of all our confusion. Up to that point our times together had been swamped with the numerous words of many active prophetic persons. There had been such an outpouring of human words, visions, opinions and convictions that we were all quite tired of listening. So we announced a fast of words from one evening to the next noon. It was a tremendous experience to see how people went out in the forest to wait upon the Lord and seek His face for what He actually wanted to say to us. Out of this experience the Lord began to give us very enlightening visions and prophetic utterances which, as I see it, turned the gathering completely around and saved it from confusion. After this day, Clifford Hill, Lance Lambert and Robert Osterman came forward with prophecies that will have a lasting effect upon the body of Christ. When all our speaking comes to an end, and when we dare to just be still and wait upon the Lord, He will never disappoint us or let us down.

When we came to the Jerusalem part of our gathering, things were pretty difficult and confused among the leadership, and it seemed as if we were all heading in different directions. I came with a strong word on my heart dealing with Jesus cleansing the Temple. The essence of my message was that judgement shall begin with the house of God. Little did I realize that that word which weighed so heavily upon my heart should turn out to become a two-edged sword that would penetrate my own heart and cut me to pieces in the following months. The very words that I spoke that night—and I believe that I received that message, however hard it was, from the Lord—came back upon my own life with tremendous force. From that evening on I entered into the most terrible time of trial and testing that I have ever undergone in my experience as a Christian.

It was when I returned to our hotel room that night that I discovered something was wrong. I could not sleep, and in the middle of the night I got out of my bed to read. When Erna, my wife, enquired what was wrong, I remember telling her that although I had been lying in bed, the most restful of all positions, I nevertheless felt as if I was riding a bike uphill. Something in my body was speeding up my system so that I could not rest. I thought the trouble must be caused by a problem with my stomach which often bothered me when I was stressed in the work. I therefore reckoned that after we returned home and took some rest everything would be okay again. I could not have imagined that for almost three years I was to walk through the furnace, and that it would almost cost me my very life.

Chapter 3

IT'S GETTING DARKER

WHEN WE ARRIVED home in Copenhagen, I began to treat my discomfort with some medication for my stomach, but it did not give me any help at all. I then thought that I would take some time off and take it very easy for a week or two, but nothing seemed to cure my physical condition. Finally, I decided to go and see my doctors.

Previously, they had never found anything wrong, but this time, after having taken an ECG of my heart, I saw them consulting each other in the corner of the room, as if they were discussing something they had found on the ECG. After a while they turned towards me, looking serious, and told me that there was nothing wrong with my stomach but that there was trouble with my heart and that as they were not able to tell me exactly what was wrong, I would have to go to the intensive care unit at the nearby hospital immediately. Since I did not consider myself to be seriously ill, fear started to grip me when they told me that I could not drive myself but would have to call my wife to come and take me to the hospital.

After some tests in the hospital, it was discovered that I was suffering from something called auricular fibrillation, causing the upper chamber of my heart to run far too fast and in irregular rhythm. None of the normal physical causes of this disease could be found, so the doctors were unable to tell me anything except the nonscientific fact that stress was the cause. They told me that this condition would reduce my energy and increase the risk of a real heart attack if it could not be cured or at least brought under control. The treatment with electric shock on the heart to make it return to its original rhythm did not work. Nor did treatment with different kinds of drugs cure my problem, but they did reduce the heartbeat. Following the initial treatment, I was told by two different doctors that I should not hope for a complete cure, since statistics showed that less than 3 per cent of patients with my kind of disease recovered fully. I could, however, look forward to a fairly normal life provided I took drugs for the rest of my days and could cope with their side-effects. Another doctor expressed the opinion that my problem was most likely due to a heart defect which I had had since my birth, but which had only recently, at the age of fifty, started to cause irregularity in the heartbeat due to the pressure I had been under, and that the 'virus' attack in Moscow had apparently triggered the whole problem. I can still hear the voice of one of my doctors: 'If we are not able to restore your original heart rhythm quickly, you are going to be a drug addict for the rest of your life.' Well, they were not able to restore it, so it did seem as if I was going to end up reducing my activities and taking a considerable number of drugs for my heart each day, which would have slowed me down in many ways. But God had other and better plans for my future life.

Shortly after leaving the hospital, things began to go really wrong. Being totally unused to the medication I was receiving, especially as I had never been ill before, I developed what is known as a chemical depression. I began to feel very tired and muddled and this, together with the fact that the disorder in the heartbeat reduced my energy by 20 per cent, soon left me open to all kinds of questions and attacks from the Enemy.

Searching for answers

I began to look inwards to find an explanation for all this. I could not understand, and felt that God was no longer hearing our prayers. I began to condemn myself, and in the end this brought me almost to the brink of self-destruction. Today I can see how the Enemy grabbed hold of the opportunity that my sickness and weakness provided in order to try to finish me off completely. At the same time I am deeply convinced that God was in this in a much stronger way than I could imagine at the time.

Situations like this are always a mixture of God's dealings and of the Enemy's mingling in order to maximize the effect of the misery. This is why it is so important to be able to discern spirits, especially when people are trying to help a sufferer. I can honestly say that I myself was not able to discern anything as the depression came upon me with increasing strength. In such a case it is all the more important that someone around you is able to make the distinction between good and evil.

Those who failed to be of real help to me were those who could not make that distinction, but claimed that everything which I went through was directly from hell, and that I should be able to resist everything and recover in no time. I would not say that any of these friends were 'friends of Job', because Job's friends did worse: they accused Job of having committed secret sins which caused his suffering. Thank God, none of those who tried to help me held that view. But some of them could not come to terms with the fact that God could be in the illness along with the fact that the devil was also active, and this became a problem for me.

Because of God's dealing with me, I was not able to respond to the various treatments which involved exercising my faith. When the therapies did not work, not even those 'handled' by some of the strongest 'faith healers', it added to my desperation and my depression because I felt guilty and more and more out of God's favour. And of course the disappointment of the friends who failed in their treatment led to their quickly giving up on me. Thus I became one of the hopeless cases who did not have faith, and therefore could not be helped.

I remember I went to see one of the best known faith preachers to ask for prayer for deliverance. He willingly prayed for me, but since his prayer at the time was without the desired effect, he accused me of being without faith. My brain still worked sufficiently for me to be able to reply: 'If I had had faith myself, I would not have been seeing you today. I know that I have no faith, but I came because I thought you had faith!'

What added to my growing depression was the fact that I, a formerly hyperactive person, was losing my energy, becoming less and less able to carry out my work. The sense of ineffectiveness and idleness weighed much more heavily upon me than my actual physical limitations. Concerning this area of my life it was clearly revealed to me that I had had my identity much more in my ministry ability than in the Lord himself. Take away the working ability, the ministry from a man, and he becomes deeply depressed if he is not deeply rooted in the Lord himself. Nevertheless, for a man the state of unemployment is a terrible thing because it hurts his manly pride far more than anything else. And here I was, walking around like a useless vegetable, having been one of the most effective and successful servants of God.

Of course, this was a natural occasion for self-examination, and it was in that process that things began to go very wrong for me. There is no doubt that God wanted to cleanse some things in my life and correct others. However, these were not of such a terrible nature that they could justify three years of torture in depression. Besides, I do not believe that God would actually punish any of his children with three years of bondage because of what I can only understand as less major sins, although of course all sin is terrible in the eyes of God because even the smaller sins caused Him to pay the greatest price—to sacrifice His only begotten Son, the Lord Jesus. And I am not sure that what we call grave sin is always measured in the same way by God, and that what we consider smaller offences also look small to the Lord. Sin in any measure and in any form is horrible and must be rejected and hated by us. But I do not believe that God punishes us in the way that I felt He was doing when I was suffering.

I admit there were sins in my life to be confessed and dealt with, and I make no excuse for that. In my pride I had allowed myself to nurture thoughts and to give myself to things that were not pleasing to God, and although I had not fallen into deeply sinful acts, I cannot justify what was there. Part of my trouble was the ongoing reluctance to heed God's continual warnings. We must suffer for being disobedient for the wages of sin is still death. Sin carries in itself a sort of punishment, just as truly as the divine law says, 'A man reaps what he sows' (Gal 6:7). It is important for us to fear sin in any form, or rather to have such a fear of the Lord that it will keep us from committing any kind of offences against His holy name. In this charismatic age, with its many blessings and benefits from God, we should never forget to teach God's people, and especially our young people, about taking sin seriously and dealing with it in true repentance.

'In all things God works'

The fact that God is in our trials and testing is a matter of utmost importance for everyone who is involved in counselling others. When considering healing it is vital to recognize God's dealings with a brother or sister before starting healing procedures. I am among those who believe in divine healing, in the fact that by the stripes of the Lord Jesus we received healing, but from my understanding of the Scriptures and the realities of life I cannot see this as being a *carte blanche* for healing in every situation and at any time.

I believe that there is a difference between talking about healing for those who are outside of Christ and those who are in Him. For the former I have much more faith for instant and unconditional healing. As far as I can see from the New Testament, most of the healings the Lord Jesus performed were worked out in the lives of unbelievers and served as signs to draw sinners into the kingdom of God. It is much more easy for me to believe for mass healing when it is directed towards the unregenerate people of this world than when we speak about those who are already in the kingdom of God, saved and justified by His grace.

I base this distinction on my understanding of God's word. Whenever anyone is in Christ he or she is under the character-building work of the Holy Spirit. God is using everything in life to mould and form us into the likeness of His own Son. This is the meaning of 'in all things God works together for the good of those who love him' (Rom 8:28). This verse in Romans is followed by one in which Paul tells us that God is working towards moulding us into the same image as His son. Therefore we can never separate whatever a born again believer is going through from the dealings of the Holy Spirit in his life. After all, God's eternal purpose is far greater than to give us a pleasant earthly life. He is concerned with our future eternal life.

Healing in the body of Christ in the New Testament is therefore linked with the process of sanctification. When Paul speaks about many being sick and some dying prematurely in the Corinthian church, he points out that the lack of healing is due to a disrespect in the church for one another. There were some broken and unloving relationships among the brothers and sisters (1 Cor 11:29–30). We cannot imagine these sick people being healed through any healing gift before they had first dealt with the broken body. In other words, we need to respect God's dealings in the lives of His dear children before we start claiming anything in terms of their instant healing. In general, believers today need to come to understand, appreciate and respect that God is a Person, and that He actually indwells the life of everyone who is truly born again by the Holy Spirit, otherwise we might contradict God's work with our well intentioned charismatic enthusiasm.

A sickness, or part of a person's sickness, can be caused directly by that person having committed a sin, but often sicknesses or physical troubles are caused, in part at least, by the fact that God is testing, purifying and sanctifying His children. We therefore need to enquire of the Lord whenever we look into the situation of one of His children.

The quicksand of despair

A point to consider about confession is that self-examination and confession of sins can be dangerous when done by people who, like me, have an oversensitive conscience. I not only made necessary confession for my sins, but I was deceived by the Enemy into confessing the same sins over and over again, so that in the end confession became almost an obsession. Every time I turned to the Lord in prayer, together with my wife, I began to go over the same mistakes and failures again and again. Finally, my wife refused to pray with me because the prayers I offered not only took away my own faith in God, but hers also.

But not only that. I began to take the blame and guilt for almost everything that went wrong, not only with myself and my family, but everything negative that happened in the church or in the work or lives of my brothers or sisters. It was all my fault. Whenever somebody was hit with problems in the fellowship, it was my fault because I was not there as the shepherd to take care of the flock. Whenever problems or heaviness occurred at a conference, it was due to the fact that I was bringing with me a spirit of depression and was unable to exercise my usual good and firm leadership.

My readiness to admit my faults may sound like real humility, but it was in fact more like pride. At that time and until I had been thoroughly broken by the Lord, I still thought that I was indispensable: God could not do without me! It was necessary for me to be around, otherwise things would fall apart.

However, the burden of taking all that upon myself, far

beyond my own sins, which I could not bear either, soon led to a terrible psychosis of condemnation, which opened the door of our home to a spirit of hell. Day and night thousands of accusations came to me, adding to my already deep depression.

At that time I began to take sleeping pills to reduce the effect of these condemning thoughts, and this developed naturally into a dependence, which gave cause for another fight. I was sinking deeper and deeper into the quicksand of utter despair. I began to think that I was no longer a Christian. If I had at any time been born again, then I had lost my salvation and was now waiting for eternal condemnation. A very strange appetite arose in my soul. I wanted to read all the passages in the New Testament that dealt with the possibility of falling out of grace.

I read them, all of them, over and over again, and I showed them to my wife in order to convince her that I was totally lost. If these scriptures, I thought and said, did not describe someone just like me, then what were they talking about? I recalled how in the old days, when I was a leader of the Young Christians Drug Addict Mission in Copenhagen, we used to speak about reaching the point of no return after some drug addict had repeatedly fallen back and finally left us to end his life.

My wife had to stand in the midst of all this. If there is one person in this world that I cherish, next to the Person of my wonderful Saviour, the Lord Jesus Christ, it is my wonderful wife. It is impossible to describe the pain and despair she had to go through. Everyone else who came to help us, and there were many, could leave after a few hours, but my wife had to stay day and night for almost three years. It is one of God's greatest wonders that she managed to come through, and it also speaks about the quality of her love for me. She actually risked her own mental health by staying with me, and a couple of times she was under such intense mental stress that she reached the point of being taken away from me.

Together with my wife, my children fought alongside

me, never giving up hope, always confessing their firm belief that one day soon I would be delivered. My son, Per, the oldest of our children, who had always felt the burden of being the son of a well known preacher, with all that carries with it, came closer and closer to me as he discovered how weak and human I was. I felt we had become knitted together in a new way when, on the last Christmas Eve before my healing, he put his hands on my head and prayed for my release. My oldest daughter, Henriette, came home all the way from Kenya, East Africa, to be with me and her mother, and was, by the grace of God, a great blessing and a comfort to us all. Anne-Christina, the youngest, was the only one of the three who was still living with us, so she got the worst of the battle. I remember how I plagued her, torturing her with my questions, and how she with great patience, (not her main virtue, nor her father's), listened to me and tried to answer, and if she could not answer she would always assure me how much she loved me, even though I had fallen into this pit.

How I thank God for my family. Friends and brothers and sisters are wonderful, but there is nothing like the Christian family, nothing like my family.

Chapter 4

THE VALLEY OF
THE SHADOW OF DEATH

URING THIS TIME of mental torture the Enemy managed to make me believe that I had actually committed the unpardonable sin: the sin against the Holy Spirit! I know it probably sounds absolutely unbelievable that a long-time preacher of the gospel, a spirit-filled, charismatic Bible teacher, a leader of a world-wide prayer movement could come that far from the truth. But the fact of the matter is that I did. Since I was unable to respond to the love being shown to me by family and friends, since there were no results of the prayers for me or of the exercise of spiritual warfare over me, and since I was apparently unchanged after many hours of counselling, there could in my estimation—and this was supported by the devil—only be one conclusion: I had committed the sin above all sins, the sin against the Holy Spirit, for which there is no forgiveness, only eternal condemnation!

When, earlier in my ministry, people I was counselling would confess their fear of having sinned against the Holy Spirit, I would always smile and tell them that the fear of that sin was a sure sign that they had not committed it, because those who had committed that sin were people who were not able to admit they had done so. The Holy Spirit would have left them, and thus they would not have felt any repentance at all. I believe that this conviction actually is correct, but just as it seemed difficult for those whom I was trying to help to believe it, so now I seemed totally unable to grasp it. That wretched demon who tortured my thoughts and emotions would not allow me to discern this deception: I really believed that I was one of the few people in this world who had committed the unforgiveable sin, and that all hope was lost.

Suicide—a way out?

It was almost inevitable that soon I began to have thoughts of suicide. Logically, when you are already lost, why not put an end to your earthly misery? More to the point, why not relieve your poor family, having tortured them so much? At least they would benefit from your departure. When God seems so unwilling to make your life worthwhile, why should you go on living? Of course, to begin with I hoped that God would somehow take me by natural death. After all, I did have some potential for sudden death. If I stopped taking the drugs for my heart, that would increase the possibility of a stroke. There have been great servants of God who, in their depressions, have wanted God to end their life and career. I can think of two: Elijah, after his great victory on Mount Carmel, and Jonah, after his disappointment in Nineveh. Both were deeply depressed by the failure of their ministry. But just as God would not respond to the pleas of Elijah and Jonah, He would not respond to mine either.

Then, for a period of approximately eighteen months, I was regularly tempted to commit suicide. If or when it happened, I hoped I could experience God's forgiveness and get out of all my misery.

I know that this revelation may shock some of my readers, and I know that I could have omitted this part of my story. I am not including it to be excessively dramatic or sensational, but to help all believers who have been shocked to discover that despite being saved they could have such temptations.

Years ago, when I was confronted with such revelations from believers, in my arrogance and pride I would reject them totally. I did not even believe that it was possible for

born again Christians to be mentally sick. I could understand physical problems to a certain degree, but never any
mental problems believers had. How could they have the
Holy Spirit within and suffer mental and even demonic
problems at the same time? And the possibility of one of
God's children committing suicide was unthinkable.

Well, I will in no way diminish the seriousness of suicide
in the eyes of the Lord, and I am not in a position to
promise anyone anything here or on the other side of
eternity. But I can say from my own recent experience that
I do understand this problem much better. I believe that it
is possible to die from a mental illness, just as death is often
the conclusion of serious physical sickness. People can actually die of depression, although I could never defend or
accept the way in which that happens. The mental faculties
of a deeply depressed person can be so worn down that that
person has no life-sustaining resources left and does not
know what he or she is doing. In such moments of extreme
mental exhaustion, death, even by one's own hand,
becomes the only way out.

One must have experienced the depths of the soul's
misery in order to hold such a view, and I believe that I
have had just that experience. All I can say today is that I
would much rather suffer from any kind of physical sickness
than such deep mental torture as I endured when I walked
down into that valley of the shadow of death. I am sure that
had it not been for God's abounding grace and mercy, I
would not be alive today.

My God, where are you?

There is another sense in which depressed people are
dying. This is a more spiritual kind of death, namely total
isolation. You may be in the company of many and have
fellowship both in your church and family and yet feel cut
off from any communication with others. What is more,
because depressed people spread an atmosphere of darkness and negativity, other people tend not to have fellow-

ship with them because they actually feel utterly helpless. For the depressed person the isolation increases. It was not at all difficult for me to identify with the words of the psalmist:

> My God, my God, why have you forsaken me?
> Why are you so far from saving me,
> so far from the words of my groaning?
> O my God, I cry out by day, but you do not answer,
> by night, and am not silent. (Ps 22:1–2).

Of course, we all know that these words came from the heart of the Son of Man when He was being forsaken by His dearly loved heavenly Father as He suffered on the cross to pay the penalty for our sins. We are aware that the actual physical death of Jesus was not the reason for His deep grief, but the fact that He was separated for a moment from the intimate fellowship with His Father. The grief and loneliness as the sins of the world were placed upon Him broke His heart and caused a quicker death than is usual for one being crucified.

I do not think it would ever be possible to describe the horror of the soul when a person feels abandoned by God and separated from His love and mercy. One would have to experience that in order to understand. 'Deep calls to deep' as the psalmist expressed it (Ps 42:7), meaning that only those who have gone through the fire can know the heat and the pain of such an experience. It also means that spiritual experience, both good and not so good, is the real basis for being able to help others. That is why it was said of our Saviour that He was tried in all things, yet without sin, that He might be able to come to the help of those who are tempted. Later in this book we will look further into this principle.

Humanly speaking, I was coming to a complete end. But somehow I was still hanging in there trying to do my job. The good point about not giving up entirely was that I could still keep in touch with people and maintain relationships, but the negative side was that I was losing my credibility in the ministry because I could only contribute what I had received before my sickness and was unable to receive anything new. What I did learn, however, was that the anointing and the gifts that God has vested in His children are still there, even when they are mentally broken. On some occasions during my sickness when I ministered there was even an unusual anointing, greater than in my days of normality.

By now, everybody, including myself, knew that things could not go on for much longer. My family's nerves were worn down, I myself was getting more and more tired and hopeless, and my friends and fellow workers in the kingdom were becoming aware of the dangers by letting me continue in my present condition. There would have to be a change if we were not all to end up in a mental institution.

Chapter 5

THE DAY I 'DIED'

A S I HAVE JUST said, up until this point I had
been able to carry out most of my duties, even if
they had been done with much less energy. Nevertheless, deep down in my heart I knew I was coming to an
end. It was just that I was not willing to quit. I feared that a
complete standstill would mean the end of my ministry and
work for ever, and that I would then finish up on the dole.

I had already done some investigation into the possibility
of going on social security. A couple of social workers in my
local district must have found it a strange experience when I
approached them and asked all the 'what...then...if...?'
questions as I tried to figure out what would happen if I
became unemployed. From what they said, my wife and I
would certainly have faced a very limited and restricted life
if we had had to let everything go, even though we were
living in possibly the best country in the world as far as
social security is concerned.

I had become too old to even hope for another job in a
country with a very high percentage of unemployment.
Also, I was somewhat physically handicapped with my
heart problem and the drugs which slowed me down. What
was even worse was the fact that I was mentally ill. Who on
earth would want to employ someone like me in the secular
world? Humanly speaking, I had no hope whatsoever for
anything other than social security.

For a man like me, at the age of only fifty, with such an
active and successful ministry behind me, this was a terrible

prospect. With it came all the shame of having to quit in terms of the bad witness it would cause. Here was one of God's servants, well known at home and abroad, known also in the world for his bold stand for the gospel and righteousness. What would all the people inside and outside the church think and say when a spiritual leader like me ended up a wreck? My mind was turning these vital questions around day and night.

It is one thing for people around to suggest that someone like me puts down everything. It is quite another thing for the one who has to do so. I am not saying that it was not right for my closest friends to insist in the end on my resignation from the ministry, only that for me it was like dying, for the reasons I have explained above. And who is in any hurry to die? But the biggest difference between those who advised me to 'die' and myself was that they believed in God and in His resurrection power, but I had lost all faith and had to face my own spiritual death without believing that there could be a new beginning.

The faithfulness of God

This matter of my having lost my faith is something that I need to explain in more depth, because it was, and to a certain extent still is, a matter of controversy. Some of my friends claimed all along that I had to exercise faith, and when I declared that I had lost it, they said that was impossible because, according to them, if I had lost my faith, I had lost my salvation.

Well to me there is no doubt that I had lost my faith, and there is also no doubt in my mind that I had not lost my salvation, although emotionally I felt so. It is my sincere conviction that we charismatic Christians have come to put too much of a load upon our own faith. As one of my friends has put it: we have come to have faith in our faith instead of faith in our God. For all of those who are going through a period of lack of faith, like I did, I have good news: God has not left any of you, just as He did not leave me. This is as true as the fact that we in our hearts have never rejected the Lord!

That it is possible for even servants of God to lose faith is known from church history. It is well known that one of the greatest missionaries of all times, Hudson Taylor, at a particular period in his work came to a complete loss of faith. He was so low that he not only thought about retiring from the mission and returning to England, but he actually wrote a letter to the mission board and asked to be released from all his duties. He had come into a strange darkness of soul from which he could see no way out. He even told some of his close friends that his whole vision and calling had been a big mistake, and that he should never have gone to China and built up the missionary ministry of faith.

One day, in the midst of this terrible situation, he was sitting having afternoon tea in his house in China. His Bible was lying there on the table. For quite a while he had not bothered to read the word of God because it did not do him any good, and only added to his despair. But, as if on impulse, he grabbed hold of his Bible and it fell open at 2 Timothy 2:13: 'If we are faithless, he will remain faithful, for he cannot disown himself.' It was if lightning had struck Hudson Taylor. As he read these words, he suddenly realized his basic mistake. He had always based everything on 'our faith', and whenever he had mentioned anything concerning his work he had always referred to it as a 'faith mission'. All the missionaries who had been sent out throughout the years had been sent 'by faith'. His whole emphasis had been on 'our faith', and that was why he had failed. Now he saw and realized that the work had to be based on God's faithfulness instead of on our faith. From that time on the whole work grew tremendously, and from then on, Hudson Taylor talked only about the faithfulness of God whenever he spoke about the mission.

'If we are faithless' can only mean that there may be times when we have no faith; when there is simply no faith left in our hearts. That does not mean that we are lost, because 'he will remain faithful'; that is, God is still full of the faith that we are lacking, because even if we change, and often do so, He can never ever deny His own self. Faith is nothing but the gift of God. It is something that is born of God into our hearts. It is not something we can stir up within ourselves as we choose and as we need it. The idea of faith as a power that can be handled at any time and in any measure, as we see fit, is unscriptural and not in accordance with the realities of Christian experience. The Lord Jesus is the Author and Finisher of our faith, the Giver, the Maintainer and the Perfecter of the faith, and to imagine that we have any faith unless we share our lives in communion with Him is wrong. We need to have the load shifted from our weak shoulders to His shoulders. There are times, and there will be times, when·it will be absolutely clear that only God's grace keeps us from falling apart, and even if we cannot hold on to Him, He will still hold on to us.

Faith is an important spiritual quality that we need to receive, but were it not for another divine quality called grace there would be no faith for us to exercise. We are told that we are saved 'by grace... through faith' (Eph 2:8), and not 'by faith through grace': God is the Initiator of everything. He is the Lord of everything. He holds us in His hands, and we dare not rely on our own understanding, experience or spiritual gifts, or the amount of faith we might possess. When at the end of my long trial I was miraculously healed, I suggested to a close friend of mine that we formed a 'grace movement' in the body of Christ. He immediately agreed to this idea, so at this time this newly formed spiritual movement has at least two members: the one who suffered God's mighty grace when all hope was lost, and the one who helped and counselled him in the very last days of his misery.

The hour of decision

But back to the point of feeling it was impossible to continue in the ministry. At the end of 1988, after two and a half years of fighting, I was still hanging on in the ring, but was severely battered and bruised. Towards the end of the year, I had an encouraging experience on a ministry tour in Austria, and I hoped that somehow the turning-point would come in time to save me from a final breakdown and having to leave the ministry. But over Christmas and New Year things got very bad. In January 1989 I was scheduled to go to England for a time of ministry. This was the third time the dear friends in Intercessors for Britain had invited me. The two previous times I had had to cancel, so this time I felt it important that I go. But it was quite clear to everybody except myself that I was totally unable to travel and minister any more.

At that time a prayer conference was being held in my church in Copenhagen. Several of my old friends and co-workers in the prayer movement were participating and ministering. I sought their advice and help, but in my heart I really wanted to get their approval for carrying on. Apparently, this was the hour of decision. These brothers, who had so patiently supported me and kept me in on their programmes, had now concluded that the time had come for me to put everything down and get away somewhere to seek healing and help. And so they would not be persuaded to support me in anything else.

It was a hard battle for me. Fear entered into my soul because I had no faith to believe what they all believed, that putting down everything before the Lord would be a major step towards healing and restoration. I finally gave in, to be honest not out of a willing heart, but because I realized that without the ongoing support of my brothers it was impossible for me to continue my ministry. That much I did understand, but like Jacob, it was as if I was giving in only when I realized that my attempt to manipulate my friends had failed.

Deeply disappointed, I looked around for one last way to save face, so that I did not have to cancel my trip to England. I began to think that maybe the drugs for my heart were making me like a zombie, and if I could only get off this heavy stuff and possibly onto something else I would recover. So I called my pastor in Sweden, Sven Nilsson, who had been a friend for a long time. He is one of the major leaders of God's work in Sweden. For many years I too had ministered there, and the Lord had knitted us together in a special way, not only in the sphere of ministry, but much more in an intimate friendship. This mature, gentle and wise man of God was the first person I consulted when all the troubles began. That is why I call him my pastor. I believe that every one of us, including God's servants, needs a shepherd whom we can consult.

Sven is an unusual servant of the Lord. Although he has great experience and wisdom, he never goes by that, but always tries to listen to what the Lord seems to say in a particular situation. I remember when, in the early days of my sickness, I visited Sven in his home near Orebro in mid-Sweden and revealed my misery to him. He gave me no straight answer, but said he would ask the Lord for a word for me. This was quite crucial for me since I could not forsee what the Lord would say and I knew that that word would decide my future destiny as a servant of the Lord.

He came back and said that the Lord had clearly given him the third chapter of Zechariah. Satan accuses the high priest Joshua, but the angel of the Lord takes him through a process of cleansing and renews him in his calling and ministry. He would not be rejected or put aside, but would in the future be allowed to have his dwelling place in the house of the Lord together with his fellow ministers. This was the word which should be fulfilled in my life, and to confirm that this was of the Holy Spirit the Lord gave me the same passage through two other channels totally independent of Sven Nilsson.

I went through a purifying process but the accusations of the Enemy were not able to remove me from the place in the sanctuary where God in his eternal elective grace had put me, together with my fellow servants. It must be a great joy for my friend Sven Nilsson today to realize that the divine counsel he gave me through God's Spirit endured throughout the years of trouble and was fulfilled in God's own time.

The morning I phoned concerning my medication, Sven listened carefully and did not rule out the possibility that there could be a problem with the drugs. He pointed out, however, that since he was not a medical doctor, he did not think he could help me on this one, and then he asked me to call another friend of mine, also called Sven—Sven Reichmann—who was not only a highly qualified medical doctor, but also one of the best Spirit filled Bible teachers in Sweden.

I had known this Sven for quite some time, and I had had the joy of being a help to him when he was in a crisis situation a few years before. For a couple of years we had not been together, but I had thought about seeking his help for my sickness, though I had never done so.

It was a Saturday morning when I phoned Sven Reichmann in Gothenburg. I just wanted to question him about the kind and the number of heart drugs I was taking every day, but when he heard my voice he could hardly recognize it and was immediately aware that something was very wrong. He then suggested that he come down to meet me, and he offered to reschedule his busy programme so that he could spend twenty-four hours in our home.

When he arrived he was pretty shocked by the change he saw in me, but he did not say much. Instead, he just listened to me. His conclusion was that I would have to be immediately released from all work and come up and stay with him and his wife, a professional nurse. They would treat my depression both medically and spiritually.

That meant, however, that I would have to cancel my trip to England. When I talked to Sven Reichmann about that, I remember I argued that it would be a step of faith to go on the trip. He then said something which I have never forgotten. He said that it would require more faith to put down everything and accept proper treatment than go on a ministry tour. It struck me that faith is seen not only in the performing of signs and wonders; the greatest expression of faith is when we are ready to 'die', to give up our own life, trusting God for His power to raise us up again to whatever He has in mind for us.

Among the faith-heroes were not only those who performed great miracles, such as conquering kingdoms and shutting the mouths of lions, but also those who were

> tortured and refused to be released, so that they might gain a better resurrection. Some faced jeers and flogging, while still others were chained and put in prison. They were stoned; they were sawed in two; they were put to death by the sword. They went about in sheepskins and goatskins, destitute, persecuted and ill-treated (Heb 11:35–37).

And yet they were reckoned as the greatest heroes of faith.

It is true that it requires more faith to suffer and to die than it does to perform great deeds. The peak of faith in Hebrews 11 is the story about Abraham sacrificing his only son by faith, laying the very fruit of his life on the altar. This act, of course, foreshadowed the greatest act of faith in all history: the Lord Jesus, God's only begotten Son, giving up His own life on the cross, not forced by anyone, but of His own free will, because He loved His Father and all of us so much!

So finally I gave in. I cannot truthfully say that I was prepared to put down my life by free will or by faith, but at least I had come to the point, pressurized by circumstances, where there was no other way. To have continued at this point would have destroyed everything, including my tortured wife and family. I therefore lifted the receiver to phone England and cancel. I had already told my wife that this would mean goodbye to ever again being invited by my British friends. When I got Ray Borlase, the director of Intercessors for Britain, on the phone I explained my situation and apologized. To my great surprise he very lovingly expressed his full understanding and promised the support in prayer of all the friends. And shortly after I even received a financial gift to help us in our situation. There was no break in relationships—that had only been a fear, put into my mind by the Enemy of souls.

Getting away from God

I shall never forget the day I left my home to go to Sven and Marianne's house in Gothenburg, Sweden, to stay for an indefinite time. As I said goodbye to my wife, I did not know when I was going to see her again, or if I was ever going to see her again. I was very low when I arrived at Sven's home.

As I walked through the door, a word came into my mind. It was just two sentences from Luke's account of Jesus' temptation in the wilderness: 'When the devil had finished all this tempting, he left him until an opportune time. Jesus returned to Galilee in the power of the Spirit' (Lk 4:13). When this word hit my mind I remember I heaved a big sigh: oh, if only that could happen to me, if only the devil would stop his torturing work for a while so that I could breathe normally and gain some strength! But I did not really believe that it would happen. I had come too far from any hope of release. Actually, I had already prepared myself to leave the ministry for ever, and to try to get better once the religious pressures had gone, and I could begin to think of myself as an ordinary human being in a secular position.

Throughout these years of trouble I often envied our neighbours, who were not even professing Christians, but who were the most delightful and sweet people you could imagine, and lived a most harmonious life. I was beginning to wonder whether trying to follow the Lord was really worthwhile, and my ambition was just to recover sufficiently to find a simple job and live a normal life with my wife for the rest of our days. I wanted no more preaching, no more living up to the high norms, no more being pressurized in the battle of spiritual warfare and in the heavy ministry of intercession, no more being concerned about nations, about evil in the world. I just wanted to live quietly, away from all the conflicts.

I no longer wanted to stagger under the burden of being so sensitive to one's conscience because of the very small margin one had as a minister of the word of God. In my heart I was even close to playing with the thought of leaving the Lord altogether and becoming a non-Christian because, after all, that could give me a much more relaxed life. At least that was what I thought, knowing, of course, deep down that once you have been called to the Lord it is not easy to run away.

The story of the prophet Jonah reveals that. Although he was not exactly leaving God altogether, he was certainly doing his best to run away from his calling and from a life in the will of God. He even payed to run in the opposite direction from that which the Lord was calling him to go. But the Lord rearranged Jonah's travel plan, and Jonah had to realize in the end that it is not at all easy to get away from God.

That would also be my experience. But I did harbour some bitterness in my heart against the Lord. I felt that He had not been treating me well, considering the fact that I had served Him faithfully throughout almost my whole life, and in a full-time capacity for nearly twenty years. How then could God allow me to suffer for so long, and not hear the prayers of so many? I knew that I had failed the Lord in some areas and that I needed discipline, but I also knew that if God intended to kill me in return for what I had done, then He would have to kill most of His servants!

The Reichmanns received me with much love and offered to let me stay for an unlimited time. They took time to talk with me whenever I felt the need, even if it was in the middle of the night. That was something I needed more than anything else, and I appreciated it greatly. Sven very kindly told me that I would be treated with a strong anti-depressant drug, and that it would make me very drowsy, especially in the beginning. I would have to accept that there would be no sign of improvement for the first couple of weeks.

Up till then I had not been willing to take drugs for my mental condition. On the contrary, I had been strongly against them. I had never seen them bring any help, and in my counselling had found that they could even make a situation worse. My healing, when it came, was such an outstanding overnight miracle that it has to be ascribed to the power of the Holy Spirit. Nevertheless, I believe that the drugs also helped.

During the treatment I came to understand that depression is not entirely of a spiritual or demonic nature, but there also is a physical side to it. The brain of a depressed person lacks an important chemical fluid which normally transmits the impulses between the different parts of the brain. The lacking chemical can be restored by drugs, and that will in many cases bring tremendous relief and at least weaken the depression. I consider that I was helped in this way and that the medical treatment led to my final deliverance. I therefore think I have to repent of my previous hard position on this issue, although I have never been among those totally opposed to a Christian taking medication.

Theologically, I see no contradiction between having faith and taking medication. I am against the overuse of drugs and the abuse and misuse of them, and I object when doctors prescribe drugs in limited quantities just to reduce a patient's misery. Sadly, these days, because of stress and pressure, doctors often have insufficient time to care for sick people or prescribe the correct medication. Often there is a lack of follow up to see how the patient is coping with his medication. Having said that, I still feel it is important to underline that the normal use of drugs is not a sign of unbelief and will not hinder the Lord from giving divine healing. Even psychiatric drugs can be useful, although they may mask the symptoms of mental illness rather than actually healing the disease.

Sven told me that I should not hope for a swift solution,

but rather expect a healing process that could take up to six-to-eight months. He said that, I believe, to prevent me from trying to give up on the whole treatment prematurely, just as if he really knew my nature. So it seemed that I had a long way to go before I could hope for release, if it was to come at all. But the Lord was soon going to set aside all my negative expectations and even the medical predictions.

God's timing

Two weeks went by without any major changes. What helped me most during that time was the willingness of Sven and Marianne to sit down and talk and pray with me, without making me feel that I needed to believe, to make progress, to proclaim or to fight. I could just rest in the assurance that even if it did not seem to help me visibly, I was not considered disqualified by them, nor did they consider their time investment in me as any big loss. I believe this, in its real essence, is the love of God, which allows us to breathe and feel relaxed, even if we are unable to show that we have improved in any way. I know from my own experience as a pastor how result-orientated we can be even in our counselling of needy people. Somehow our busy schedules do not allow us to spend time with those who come to us and just be with them without expecting significant things to happen. We consider everything which does not produce results more or less instantly as a waste of precious time, not realizing that God came to be with us, not in the first place to obtain results, but to identify with us in our great need.

Naturally, I am not talking about situations where people just want to take advantage of the pastor's time. Such people should be silenced. But in counselling we must somehow be able to transmit to our friends in need that we do love them, and that assurance is very often manifested to them by our having sufficient time to spend with them. The Reichmanns did not spend the time going through a lot of spiritual therapies with me. I had done that already, and it had not helped me. We were just together before the Lord in prayer and worship and no attempts were made to reach certain presupposed conclusions.

What a marvellous treatment this was for me. Patience and love was the 'medicine' that began to restore my hope of getting back to normal again. The very thought, too, of God's timing of things was very helpful, although difficult to accept. Years ago I learned a little chorus that contains a very important truth: 'God does all that He will in His own time!' It is hard to learn to wait upon God. Certainly, I had to wait longer than I was naturally able to before healing came to me. I am not suggesting that everybody else would have to wait as long as I did, but I do believe that part of the healing process is to learn to be patient and wait for God's time. After all, the promise to Abraham was fulfilled through 'faith and patience': not only faith, which here could mean 'action', but also patience, which means 'waiting'. Those 'who wait for the Lord shall renew their strength' (Is 40:31, RSV). We cannot explain why it is that we have to wait for the Lord. It is one of the mysteries. However, in my case it became clear later on why the Lord would not give me instant healing. There was something He had to let happen in my life before I was able to benefit from His healing power.

An honest heart

Time went by in the house up there on the west coast of Sweden as I continued with my treatment. Although I did feel some physical improvement because I was under better medical care and control, I did not feel better spiritually. On the contrary, I was going downwards.

Two weeks after my arrival it was Friday, 24th February 1989. This day turned out to be the most terrible day in my fifty years of existence. In the morning the Reichmanns left for work, and I was then alone. This was the time when I gave up. In the afternoon I cried and wept for two whole hours, calling upon the Lord for help to get me out of this pit. It was my last outburst of anger and bitterness. I felt like going out into the kitchen to use one of the large knives on myself. Everything within me was a total emotional mess and I knew I had come to an end. I remember I told the Lord that if He really wanted so much to get rid of one of His servants, then I could no longer resist Him in that. I was going to give up totally.

That afternoon I felt like Abraham, when he took his young boy Isaac up the mountain to offer him as a burnt offering before the Lord. I had come to the point where I was finally going to lay down my ministry and calling and never again try to uphold it through my own effort. Actually, I had no choice any more. Even if I had wanted to go on, I simply could not have done so. I was finished. Therefore my 'sacrifice' was no sacrifice in the sense that Abraham's was. It was more like Jacob receiving the final touch on the socket of his hip in his battle with the angel of the Lord.

Nevertheless, I did use the words of Abraham in my last battle with the Lord. I told the Lord that I would lay down my life and ministry on the altar, and that I would lift the knife and kill it—He was the only One who could prevent me from doing this, and restrain my hand, as He did with Abraham. If He did not intervene before the next morning, Saturday, 25th February, I would sit down at my typewriter and write my letters of resignation to both the local church in Copenhagen, where I was still employed as pastor, and to the board of directors for Intercessors International, whom I served as the international co-ordinator. I would have no choice but to leave every aspect of spiritual work and to go on social security until I could come to find some other kind of work. I can honestly say that I was deeply serious about this, and also that I did not imagine I would ever again come to serve God in His house.

This was the hour in which I began to blame God for His seeming lack of interest in my case. I felt like departing from Him because He had allowed me to become a laughing-stock. My life had ended as a contradiction to everything I had so boldly preached, and everybody around me had reason to ask, 'Where is his God?' If this was the way God wanted it, then He was going to have it that way, but He should no longer count on me. I would be miles away from Him and His kingdom if this was the way He was going to treat His servants. Yes, there was rebellion in my heart. Because of my deep mental trouble I am sure God must have classified my reaction like this: 'Forgive him since he does not know what he is doing'!

Let me comment on this issue. I do not think God is afraid of having us speak our minds to Him, even when we disagree with Him over the things He is doing or allowing to happen in our lives. I have often admired Jonah, not for His rebellion against God's will, but for his outspokenness. I admire God for letting him do that without calling fire down from heaven to consume him. Jonah actually responded to God's calling with a clear-cut, 'No Sir!' But I believe he did it out of deep ignorance and religious prejudice. God did not destroy him for that, but did correct him.

Jonah also reacted bitterly to the way God 'cheated' him by not fulfilling the prophecy he had given concerning Nineveh, but instead forgave the city. He actually argued with God that he had been right to assume from the beginning that God would not carry through His word of judgement; that was why he, Jonah, had fled from the assignment. Jonah felt God had not been logical in what He had been doing. In reply to this accusation the Lord only asked if Jonah really felt that He should not show mercy to all these people, now that they had repented properly.

God does not despise an honest heart and mind. He is, I believe, much more against religious pretence and hypocrisy. Again, God can better tolerate those who are cold, although He much prefers those who are warm. The lukewarm are disgusting in the eyes of God. He promised that He would spit them out of His mouth. It is much better to tell God how we feel than to try to pretend that everything is all right when in fact we are displeased with the Lord.

In some way I felt a sense of release that Friday night when I had made up my mind, told the Lord how I felt, and was prepared to resign my positions and leave religious life altogether. Some pressures left me, but I was terribly exhausted and decided to take some extra sleeping pills to help me sleep through the night and way into the next morning—the morning of the first day when I would no longer be God's servant. Only something most unusual would now be able to change the course of my life, something miraculous.

Chapter 6

THE SAINTS ARE THE GLORIOUS ONES

S INCE MY HEALING it has been my constant testimony that it was a sovereign move of God, and no person, least of all myself, was involved. We had all given up our own efforts. I know such a statement sounds very Calvinistic, but that part of Calvinism which puts the load on the Lord and ascribes all the power and glory to Him is true and biblical, and all God's children must accept it, including we charismatics, who rely so much on the powerful gifts and manifestations of the Spirit. I have come to believe very much in the sovereignty of God, and have found a whole new trust, freedom and joy in the Lord because I now know that He holds the key and the power, even when we are in trouble and are unable to hold on. This does not mean, however, that our responsibility to respond and obey is ruled out. In my healing story some very special people played an important role, although none of them was able to pull me through in the end. These children of the living God endured with me in love and prayer. The greatest support came from my wonderful wife and three children, who suffered with me right through to the end, to the point where most of the others had given up.

Family love

My wife Erna is a very special person. I nearly said she has to be in order to cope with someone like me. She has never been among the outspoken and outgoing women in the church. She really prefers not to be in the limelight, and she is not keen on any kind of spiritual feminist movement in the church. In that she just happens to agree with her husband, although I have never tried to influence her in that direction. She just wants to fall in line with the biblical perspective of what it is to be a woman, a wife and a mother, and she has never believed that we in our modern day need to improve or modernize God's clear and unmistakable word. She used to tell me that in the end we would all come to understand that God is wiser than we are.

My wife really fits these words of the apostle Peter:

> Your beauty should not come from outward adornment.... Instead, it should be that of your inner self, the unfading beauty of a gentle and quiet spirit, which is of great worth in God's sight. For in this way the holy women of the past who put their hope in God used to make themselves beautiful. They were submissive to their own husbands (1 Pet 3:3–5).

No one should think my wife is weak and wavering. She was born on Bornholm, an island in Denmark which is also known as the 'Rock Island', and I can testify how much of the character of the real Rock, the Lord Jesus, I have found in my wife. By the grace of God she passed the most severe testing through fire and came out without even the smell of scorching.

The first year or so of our trial was extremely difficult for her, and the darkness in me brought her twice to the brink of a mental breakdown. We seriously considered the possibility that she might have to go away from our home for mental treatment. I called the leader of our church and his wife to come to us. They stayed at our house for hours embracing my wife and praying for her. Suddenly she came out of her pent up state, and we were able to avoid hospital treatment.

When it was darkest, the Lord gave my wife the faith of Abraham. You remember how Abraham was able to trust in God and believe in His promises when the promise concerning the birth of a son seemed utterly impossible. All of a sudden Erna displayed a firm belief that I would come through in the end and be healed. From that moment on nothing could alter her deep trust in God, and eventually her faith were rewarded beyond imagination.

What then can I say? No other person in our situation suffered as she did, not even myself. Depressed people are to a certain extent protected by the fact that in their mental distress they are unable to register the reality about themselves. They do not know how far they are out of themselves. That is why the most dangerous period in terms of suicidal actions is when the depressed person is on his way out of the darkness, and is beginning to come to his senses and realizing how sick he is. To be the closest person to a mentally ill partner, living with him for twenty-four hours a day for nearly three years, is suffering beyond comprehension. Erna kept on loving me and staying by my side, and in addition to coping with me she had to see to the affairs of our family. By the grace of God she managed all that, and our love and friendship grew.

When a man is going down, as I did, one of the most hurtful things is his fear of losing his image of being a good father to his children. When I think back to these years of pain I remember how much sadness I felt because my children could see their great preacher father in such a state of fear and self-pity. I was afraid that they would lose all respect for me, both as a servant of God, but more particularly as their father. I would weep in front of them, begging for their prayers and torturing them with the many questions that I expected them to be able to answer, but afterwards I felt so ashamed, and thought I had lost all respect. For them to see this previously strong and confident man, of whom they used to be so proud, wailing and yelping like a whipped dog, was a tremendous blow to my manly pride.

But all my fear was groundless. Both Per, my son, and Henriette and Anne-Christina, my two daughters, kept telling me throughout this long time that they still loved me, and what is more, that it was a moving experience for them to see that their father, this well known preacher, was just another human being, as weak as anyone else. And so we found a deeper fellowship, no longer based on ability and success in life, but on the brokenness of heart, on the humility which comes from having been stripped of everything. Of course, they had no way of meeting my intellectual needs in terms of explaining why I had to go through all this, but their constant love and support, no matter how I was, was one of the things which sparked a flame of hope deep down in my innermost being. I praise God for my family. Without their ongoing love and support I would not have been able to make it.

The power of prayer

As many of you know, I have been engaged in prayer ministry for several years, and so I, more than some, have learned to appreciate the power of intercessory prayer. In my short lifetime I have witnessed nations and governments being shaped and changed through the interceding prayers of God's people all over the world, something that compelled me to make prayer a high priority in my ministry. And then I, the leader of one of the great prayer movements in the world, ended up in a situation where I could not even pray for my own personal deliverance.

This fact actually became a stumbling-block for some of my friends in the Christian world. How could the leading figure of a prayer movement sink so low? And why couldn't he pray himself into freedom, when he had been able to pray so powerfully for nations and much bigger issues? Although I have to admit that they were right, I did feel that their attitude was much like that of Job's friends, who kept on questioning Job's motives and undermining his trust in God. Well, I hold nothing against these few who out of ignorance spoke like that. In the mighty healing move of God I was totally delivered from all bitterness towards anyone.

But I would like to issue a word of caution here to everyone who is dealing with depressed people. If you do not know what to say, and if the Lord has not given you the key to release your troubled brother, then please do not say anything. Do not become a 'friend of Job'. Your troubled brother does not need that kind of a friend. He has enough to confront in battling with all the enemies of his battered soul. Do not join the 'Accuser of the brethren', who accuses them day and night. If your method or therapy does not seem to work, please do not blame the patient. Look instead at your own failure to help and seek the Lord for better answers to the need of the person who cannot help himself in his deep distress and misery.

No method or therapy tried on me helped. That is not to say that they cannot or will not work on others, but as far as I am concerned, I have stopped believing in any sort of set method. I believe in God as a living Person. But even if these things did not work, I am deeply convinced that all the prayers, even the smallest and most feeble one aided my release. God is very fond of the prayers of His saints. He has two special interests: the prayers of His people and the tears of His saints.

In chapter 8 of Revelation we are told that the prayers of the saints are being stored in golden bowls before the throne of God. Mixed with the incense of the Holy Spirit, in due time they are poured out upon the earth, causing tremendous revolutionary changes to take place. It is most encouraging to realize that no prayer from an honest heart is lost, but is being kept and turned by God into a powerful move in the history of mankind.

When I was finally delivered by the power of God it was as if one of these bowls of divine explosives was being emptied and poured out upon me, driving my enemies away. I was most fortunate in that people of God all over the world prayed for me throughout the entire time I was walking down that dark tunnel. I received letters and phone calls confirming that I was on the prayer-lists of many individuals, groups and churches around the world. The different intercessory conferences being held around the globe throughout the year included me in their subjects for prayer. How could I but end up experiencing the grace of God? In a very special way I remember that when there was nothing else that I could hold on to in my great need, I would often tell the Lord that He would have to do something about my situation because He could not possibly ignore all these prayers being sent up for me. If I suffered attacks of evil because I had carried leadership responsibility for the worldwide prayer movement, then I also received massive worldwide prayer support from my fellow intercessors. In the long run, the prayers of the saints outweighed the accusations of the devil.

In particular, I would find myself reminding the Lord about an elderly sister, Sofia Jorgensen, who had been the most faithful intercessor in my life and ministry. I knew that sister Sofia had prayed for me every day for some thirty-three years. I first met her one Sunday morning in 1955, when I attended a worship service in a Christian fellowship in Copenhagen. I shall never forget what happened. After the service I was approached outside the church by sister Sofia. She shook my hand and said only this: 'Young brother, from now on I will pray for you every day, that you might give yourself to serve the Lord!' That was all. Little did I realize at that time what was going to happen to me. From that time on a power of God came upon my life, often hindering me from going astray and leading me slowly but surely in the ways of the Lord, until one day I found myself in full-time service for the Master.

Another prayer which was fulfilled was that my dear mother prayed for me when I was still in her womb: that I would become a servant of the Lord!

Often during the time that Sofia was praying for me she would be prompted by the Spirit to call me and inquire about my situation. Each time I wondered how she knew about me being in great need at that particular hour. Sofia died at the age of 102. For several years at the end of her life she was confined to her bed and wanted more than anything to go to be with the Lord, but in spite of her utter weakness she was still kept down here. People used to wonder why she could not be allowed to see the face of her Saviour. I didn't. I knew she was being kept down here for the sake of me and the many others for whom she interceded. In the darkest hour of my trial I would cry out to the Lord and tell Him that there was no way He could ignore this great investment of prayer that Sofia had made on my behalf. How would He be able to explain to her that thirty-three years of daily intercession had been wasted? He couldn't, and He didn't! He was only waiting for that moment when His purposes were fulfilled.

Friendship in action

Then there were the two Svens of Sweden, whom the Lord used as midwives to bring me through into new life. Sven Nilsson and his dear wife Solveig gave me ongoing counsel all the way through, without getting tired of my unchanged condition. As my personal pastor he still believed the word he had received concerning me, although all the odds seemed to be against it. He was absolutely sure he had heard the voice of the Spirit and he was relentless in his pursuit of the goal the Lord had set before us. He and Solveig prayed continually for us. They also took our needs to the prayer team of co-workers in the Vastanaas Christian Centre, of which Sven was the leader. I believe I managed to exasperate Sven only once, when I kept insisting that I was lost in spite of God's word that I was not. It is incredible how a depressed person can come to love darkness almost more than the light, just as if he has no other identity left than his own misery and is trying to hide himself in it. I remember how firm the altogether gentle and patient Sven then became, and I believe that the firmness he showed in believing in God's promises somehow caused a turn about in my heart. Many would have given up long before that, and some did give up on me, but never Sven. I do believe that his trust in the Lord on my behalf and his trust in me also was something that kept me from falling apart and kindled the small fire of hope that was deep inside of me.

The other Sven and his lovely wife Marianne became as it were my last resort in the three years of struggle. They are both deeply convinced Lutherans, although they love all God's people and serve and minister among them. But something about this Lutheran foundation, mixed with a Spirit filled life, became a real help to me. They did not suffer from the usual Pentecostal impatience or demand instant results. They were calm and quiet about everything. For me this was like the balm of Gilead upon my hectic soul. Somehow I could identify with them deeply. The Lutheran way of believing in God's grace and in the cross of the Lord Jesus has always appealed to me, although I have a Pentecostal background. It could be connected to the fact that my family on my father's side were for the last 400 years strongly Lutheran, with two Lutheran priests included among them, all from the well known city of Weimar in Eastern Germany.

I also found in Sven's and Marianne's attitude that Germanic quality of still believing in the value of a good mind. Sven, being a well qualified medical doctor in the field of radiology, used to analyze things. Although filled with the Spirit, he still believes that there is a place for a good and sound mind in the spiritual life, and I agree with him in that very much.

Despite what I have said, I make no attempt to glorify Lutherism. I know how much falling away from the truth there has been in the Lutheran denomination. But it is important for Pentecostal people to become more rooted in the fundamental truths of the gospel, and not just fly high in the Spirit. Just as legalism and dogmatism have been a problem in the church, so the lack of foundation in God's word has been a problem among charismatics.

What was so beneficial for me in my dealings with Sven Reichmann was that I could talk sense with him. We could argue and reason about things, and he was able to understand my analytical mind. Nevertheless, Sven was the one who helped me to come to see God's sovereignty in a deeper way.

I shall never forget one of the lessons. We were talking one day about the strange fact that God accepted Abel's sacrifice, but turned away the sacrifice of Cain. Sven raised this matter in the form of a wondering question, a kind of mystery that could not be explained. I reacted to that and informed him that I actually knew what was the reason for God's acceptance of Abel and his rejection of Cain, and then I began to unfold my theological theory. You see, I am one of those who have an answer to every biblical problem, or at least I used to be. I am no longer so sure about it. But Sven said, 'No, you don't know, because the Scripture does not say, and so your explanation cannot be supported as truth.' And he continued by saying that when God does not explain a thing to us then we do not know, and the correct biblical answer to the problem quite simply is: we don't know! And that is no disaster because we need to realize that God is greater than us and that His mind is bigger and much more brilliant than ours. If we were able to understand everything God said or did, He would no longer be God!

Oh, how that helped me in my furious reasoning to find the answers to my suffering, and in the suffering I endured listening to all those who claimed they had the answers. For the first time I began to realize that although I did not understand in depth what was happening to me, and probably never would, God still had me and my situation in His hands and had everything under control. How different this kind of counsel was to that of Job's friends, who had figured out everything about God and God's dealings with His servant.

How I thank God for these two men of God and for the

wisdom and maturity given by God which enabled them to stand with us all the way through until the day of victory.

And then there are, of course, my brothers on the board of Intercessors International: John Beckett (USA), Lance Lambert (Jerusalem) and Noel Bell (Australia), who all in spite of the geographical distances were a tremendous help and encouragement.

John, who is the chairman of Intercessors for America, would call me regularly from the States to be updated on our situation, and through this long period of three years, when I was good for nothing from a working point of view, he would make sure that we were financially supported all the time. Had I been employed by a secular firm, I might have been sacked within the first couple of weeks of my sickness. But not so in the kingdom of God. How wonderful it is whenever the kingdom of God prevails upon this earth, and how different everything is when the love of God is involved. I do not know how many flowers were sent to my wife and me from John and his wife Wendy through our years of pain.

John, who is on the organizational side of Intercessors International, never once suggested the possibility of me resigning from my position, although he was well aware of my incapacity. Neither did my superiors or any of the others ever make such a suggestion, but always assured me that I was God's choice for this job, and whenever I suggested to them that I should resign, they refused to listen. It was marvellous to see the outstanding character of these three brothers whom the Lord had given me on the board.

Lance has been a friend of mine for a long time. I believe that we have known one another for almost thirty years, ever since I began to visit the Christian fellowship in Richmond, near London, where Lance had been instrumental in building up a unique local church. It was through men like Lance, who always majored on prayer, that I became motivated for the ministry. I know how much Lance and his young brothers, who helped him in his house in Jerusalem, interceded for me while I was sick, and I shall never forget his reaction one day when I phoned him just to let him know that I was worse than ever. 'But we have been praying for you in our daily prayer time every day!'

Lance was probably the only one who was able to discern my trial in the right way. Unlike so many others who wanted to raise my expectations by giving encouraging promises of imminent deliverance, I remember that Lance very clearly told me I should not expect any speedy solution because he felt from the Lord that my trouble was a 'thorn in my flesh' and was serving some purpose of God in my life. In his counsel to me he pointed out that although I did not feel it, the Lord was present with me in my sufferings, just as much or maybe even more than in my good days. He quoted the experience of the psalmist: 'If I make my bed in the depths, you are there!' (Ps 139:8). A most remarkable thought.

He then told me about a missionary whom we both used to know who, for several years, emotionally felt as if she was living in hell, and yet experienced the presence of the Lord in the midst of it all, until she later came out from her darkness into the light. Through this I began to understand that God actually was much more in my situation than I had thought, and that I was suffering not only because of my own foolishness, but also because of some purposes God had for my ministry.

One day, when we were having one of our international prayer conferences in Jerusalem, I suffered a breakdown right in the middle of my speech. Brother Kjell Sjoberg stood up, threw his big arms around me and said in Swedish, 'Johannes, you must know how much we all love you!' After the meeting Lance said to me, 'Johannes, you are a prophetic sign!' Well, at first I did not know whether I should feel honoured or further depressed by his statement. If I was being specially tried, my tendency would be to react as the Jews do when they are told that they are God's special, elected people. To the Jewish mind election is often linked with suffering, so they therefore want to relinquish their special position and become just like any other

73

people. In *The Fiddler on the Roof*, the Jewish father suffering endless harassments suddenly turns to God and bursts out, 'Couldn't you just for a change choose somebody else!' However, it is true: it is terrible to fall into the hands of the living God, and our God is a 'consuming fire'.

Nevertheless, I began later to understand what Lance was pointing to. What I was going through in this fire of refinement and purification foreshadowed in a small way the furnace of affliction waiting for both the church and the people of Israel in the last days. There is a fire that will burn in every person's life in order to test the quality of one's work, whether it is wood, hay and stubble, or gold, silver and precious stones. And the sooner we can go through that process, the better, because that will give us time to cleanse and correct that which is of no spiritual value in our lives and ministries.

At the conference, Lance had been carrying around a word in his spirit, without knowing for whom it was meant. When I broke down, he knew, and he stood up and quoted the word from Isaiah 54:11–14:

> O afflicted city,
> lashed by storms and not comforted,
> I will build you with stones of turquoise,
> your foundations with sapphires.
> I will make your battlements of rubies,
> your gates of sparkling jewels,
> and all your walls of precious stones.
> All your sons will be taught by the Lord,
> and great will be your children's peace.
> In righteousness you will be established:
> Tyranny will be far from you;
> you will have nothing to fear.
> Terror will be far removed;
> it will not come near you.

Needless to say, this word put into perspective all that I was going through. How it comforted my soul to know that by God's grace and mercy all the painful things would be used to produce some precious stones in my character. Now that it is all over, though not God's ongoing dealings, because they continue throughout life, I can see how accurate Lance's picture of my situation was.

As I have already said, I am most fortunate in having been privileged to walk with a great team of God's men, who included me in their schedules and let me be a part of the work we had been involved in together, even when I was so sick that I could not possibly have been anything but a burden.

Noel Bell, the third man on our board, who has a strong, impulsive nature, found it difficult to discern what I was going through at the beginning of my illness, but as we met in Singapore for the biannual prayer leaders' conference, he undertook for me by assuming the organizational leadership, together with his dear wife and daughter, which was my responsibility. And a little later, as we together participated as observers at a global consultation conference, also in Singapore, Noel took me to his heart as a father, loving me and praying with me at all times around the clock. A very warm relationship developed between the two of us, and a most remarkable thing happened when the Lord finally raised me up.

Some days after my healing I received a letter from Noel. He told me that he had had a very special experience in the Spirit when he was praying one day for me. A powerful sense of assurance about my release came upon him, and he was lifted up in the Spirit and began to speak out my healing with great conviction. In his letter he repeated the very words that he had proclaimed in the Spirit, and told of the great joy that had filled his soul, making him shout hallelujahs and amens over and over again. I recall from his letter that he proclaimed that I was free *now!* When I calculated the time of his experience and compared it with the time difference between Sydney, Australia, and Gothenburg, Sweden, I discovered the amazing fact that the Lord's healing hand came upon me at the very same moment that Noel spoke out what he saw in the Spirit! And we were as far away geographically as two people could possibly be.

I was reminded of the event in the Gospels when a nobleman came to Jesus to ask for healing for his sick son, and Jesus just said, 'You may go. Your son will live' (Jn 4:53). When he returned he found that the healing of his son had taken place at the very hour that Jesus had spoken these words. How encouraging it is to know that in the Spirit and in the life of prayer there are no time differences and no geographical distances. Although separated in the flesh by thousands of miles, we have the glorious ability to fellowship in God's Spirit, a foretaste of our future life when we shall receive our resurrection bodies.

There were many others, like Gustav and Elsa Scheller, very dear friends of ours, who kept phoning us, supporting us throughout the whole period of my sickness. Gustav even came all the way to Copenhagen to see me and to pray and encourage us. He never stopped telling me that their love for us had not ceased, but rather had increased ever since they had learned that I had fallen ill.

Steven Lightle kept me in his heart and prayers and also kept inviting me to join him in his ministry. We had travelled together in the Soviet Union and in so doing learned to trust our lives to one another. Steve's love and compassion, because he truly is a man of love, was balm on our wounds.

Then there were Kjell and Lena Sjoberg. In the intercessory prayer work there has probably been no one that I worked so closely with as Kjell, although two persons on earth could hardly be so different. Kjell and Lena gave me hospitality for a week in their Stockholm flat, and invited me to be a part of the team many times through my years of pain.

The same can be said about Rolland and Carrie Smith from St Louis in the USA. I shall never forget how they invited me to come over and be a part of the citywide St Louis prayer conference, and I just wonder what they got out of it in terms of ministry help. But in their house we fought the battle together, sometimes both day and night. Rolland kept telling me that whatever it was I was going through, he firmly believed that it was to prepare me for an even greater ministry in the future. He took me around seven European capitals on the great prayer tour which changed so much in the body of Christ throughout the whole continent.

Two of the friends who were closest to us are today sharing the ministry here in Altensteig, Germany. Berthold and Barbara Becker, leaders of Intercessors for Germany, came to play a major role in our recovery. Berthold counselled me many times over the phone, and we often had prayer meetings on the telephone. He kept me informed of all the ongoing arrangements in Germany, where, in 1980, we had launched Intercessors for Germany which, by God's grace, has become one of the strongest national prayer movements in the world. When we started out in 1980 we had twenty-five participants in our German national prayer conference. In 1989 more than 400 intercessors participated in the national conference, and we had with us several of the key charismatic leaders in the land.

Barbara Becker had a very vivid dream one night during my sickness. She saw me standing like a general in military uniform with two stars on my shoulders. Suddenly a dark hand grabbed hold of my shoulders, trying to rip off one of the stars. After a fierce fight it became clear that the dark power would not be able to succeed, and then she saw me smiling, with a third star added to my general's uniform. The interpretation was not difficult. The Enemy was trying to finish me off, but he would not succeed, and after the fight I would be entrusted by the Lord with even greater responsibility in His army. At the time she had the dream and told me about it I was unable to believe it. I would have been happy to come out of the battle able to carry on as a corporal or even a private. But everything in that dream has had its fulfilment, and today, by God's grace and through the prayers of so many of God's dear people, I am able to continue the ministry in an enlarged way.

Many others also blessed us with their prayers and by sending letters and phoning us from all four corners of the world. We received many encouraging words, all promising us that God had not forgotten us or given up on us, but was going to bring us through in the end.

Last, but in no way least, there were the brothers and sisters from our local church in Copenhagen, a church that I was instrumental in forming in 1974, together with two other brothers, Kjeld and Anni Mikkelsen, the couple who took over the leadership of the church after me, together with a small group of close friends, helped us and showed us much love. Often they would come to pray for us in our home. They did much, but in the end they despaired somewhat, finding that I did not respond. There was a major problem. Our local friends had been under my ministry for several years and I had become like a spiritual father to them. Now, when they saw me in deep misery, unable to function with my former strength and authority, they found it very difficult to be my counsellors. It was just as if the children were trying to help and correct a parent. It became clear that I needed to be under the counsel of some who, like myself, had been in the ministry for years. That is why today I recommend very strongly that all God's servants have a pastor from among their own circle and with sufficient spiritual experience and maturity to be able to relate to their problems.

Chapter 7

FIVE O'CLOCK IN THE MORNING

NOW BACK TO the day I 'died'. The 24th February 1989 will always remain the most terrible day of my life—the day when I fought the last battle and lost, having to give up and lay down my 'Isaac', the calling of God upon my life, the ministry I had cherished so much for the last twenty years. And there was quite a lot to put down. Seen from a purely human point of view, it was no wonder that I broke down. At that time I was holding my seven different spiritual leadership responsibilities, and that is enough to knock out anyone who takes his work seriously. I was the senior pastor of the local church, the leader of Intercessors for Denmark, and also the international co-ordinator for Intercessors International, a global network of some forty nations. Besides that, I was a member of the Swedish Exodus ministry team, taking teaching ministry into the Eastern European countries, and also a member of the editorial board of the Swedish magazine called *Exodus*, which involved me in quite a lot of work, writing feature articles and columns. Then I had the role as one of the chief advisers to Women Aglow in Denmark. And finally I had a widespread Bible teaching ministry among churches within the spiritual renewal in Scandinavia, which often involved travel. As I have already said, not all these roles were equally heavy, but put together they were far more than a single person could possibly undertake without running into serious trouble. Because I was a very tense character and also ambitious in carrying out my business, it was only a matter of time before some kind of breakdown or burn out would hit me.

And now the lot had been put down. A mixture of release and deep disappointment filled me as I lay down in my bed to sleep into the first day of what I believed would be a new secular life. I had no hope whatsoever for a turn around at this late hour. I did not believe God was interested in anything but dismissing me from the ranks of His servants. I felt disqualified, like a horse taken out of the race and put to grass, just waiting to die. How could God do this to me? And if it was not God's doing, how could He allow the devil to do it? I did not know, and I had also come to the point where I did not care. I was getting out of the religious phase of my life, wondering of course what would be in store for me in the future.

The extra sleeping pills I had taken that night made me drift away from all these speculations into no man's land, where I hoped to be long into the morning of the following day.

Resurrection morning

To my great surprise I woke up at a few minutes to five in the morning with the sense that something unusual was going on within me. Although still not quite awake, I remember I sat up in my bed looking around to see if there was someone in my room. It could be the house cat, who now and again would sneak in to investigate. But there was no one, not even the cat. Then I had this strange feeling that the early morning hours were quite different from those during the last three years. The real nightmare of my life would be the early hours of the morning, when the accusations and the condemnation would come upon me with a tremendous force, making me wish that I had never woken up. It is a well known fact among depressed people that the morning is the horror of their existence.

But this morning things were different, and before I could even register what was so different and why, I felt as if a hand was laid upon my head and I became very hot. We old-time Pentecostals used to speak about a hot stream going through our bodies whenever we experienced some healing. This was what I felt. It was as if my two big toes had been put into the light socket on the wall. I became extremely hot all over for about thirty seconds, and after that three years of endless depression, accusation and condemnation vanished away like dew before the first rays of the rising sun.

As an almost automatic reflex action I moved my hand over my chest to discover that my heart rhythm was back to normal. It was then I knew that someone was in my room, although I could see no one with my physical eyes, and that someone was the Lord Jesus. One thirty-second laying on of His wonderful hand had ended three years of suffering and torture.

I know it was the Lord, because He spoke very clearly to me for the next ten minutes, and the light that flooded my soul was so bright that it not only covered all in the past, but gave me enough spiritual light for the rest of my life. All the Scripture verses and portions that I had received over these last three years came alive and made eternal sense to me, just as if a button had been pushed on some hidden computer file and the whole program lit up on the screen.

Step by step the Lord explained all that I had been going through, not so much explaining 'why' as 'what for'. I am beginning to understand that our God is a God of divine purpose and destiny. He does not very often explain why, but He rather outlines for what purpose things have happened in our lives, and how He in His grace and mercy is making all things work for good.

To me it was nothing less than being raised from the dead, a resurrection following the death of my own power and strength. It was a miracle, and its dramatic outworking is certainly the most powerful spiritual experience I have ever had, including my new birth and the baptism of the Holy Spirit. So remarkable was the change that it was hard for people to really believe what had happened, and it took almost eight months before I had absorbed the power of God and come back to a more 'normal' state. The presence of Jesus was so powerful that I am deeply convinced I could not have stayed alive much longer in that consuming light and fire.

People have asked me if it would not have been wonderful to have gone on in that manifested presence of the Lord for the rest of my life. But my answer is, 'No way!' The glory of the Lord is such concentrated light and power that we in our mortal bodies will not be able to stand that presence for much longer than a few minutes. Why do you think the apostle John fell down as dead when the Lord revealed Himself to him and he beheld the Lord? And why do you think that Isaiah, when he received that vision of the Lord seated on the throne in His holiness, cried out, 'Woe to me! I am a man of unclean lips' (Is 6:5). Moses wanted to behold the glory of the Lord, but the Lord warned him that this would cost him his life, because no man can see God and live. Therefore God in His mercy let Moses see a glimpse of His glory from behind, when He passed by him.

When people tell me that they see the Lord here, there and everywhere, and that the Lord is visiting them almost every other night, I find it very hard to believe. If it were so, I think they would have been dead long ago. I think that they are talking more about things in their imagination. I believe we should be more careful not to deflate the majesty of God's glory and of His manifest presence. I know I could not have endured much more of the Lord's power that morning, and I did not even see the Lord. I felt His hand upon me and I heard Him speak as I have not heard Him before in all my life.

As I realized I had been delivered, and after the Lord had left me, I jumped out of bed and ran down the stairs into the kitchen, where Sven and Marianne were sitting at the breakfast table, because Marianne had to leave early for work. As I burst through the door with the joy and glory of the Lord on my face, Sven looked over his glasses with the puzzled gaze of a medical researcher as if he was trying to figure out whether I had gone completely mad. Then he said in a very convincing voice, 'Johannes, this cannot be the drugs, this must be the Lord!' And then all three of us began to laugh. This was the first laugh from me in three long and heavy years.

Light, freedom, joy and peace flowed like a river through my soul. God had met me, when all was finished and hopeless. He had raised me up from the grave and given me a totally new life. I never have been able, and never shall be able, to describe the feelings, the wonder of being whole, sane and sound!

My wife was the first to know. I phoned her, but at first it was hard for her to believe that I had been delivered. Although she rejoiced over the fact that I was singing a different melody than before, she still feared that it was not real. Three years of having to cope with darkness and terror had made her build up her defences. Only when she came some days later and saw for herself could she accept that a miracle had happened.

Freedom in the Spirit

I shall never forget the day after my healing. I went to the Lutheran church together with Marianne. My spirit was so sensitive that I was weeping, not for pain, but for joy, as we sang the good old hymns, and the sermon went right to my heart. Almost every word pierced my spirit and I was able to hear God's voice with a clarity I had never possessed before, not even before my sickness. The way my spirit was able to communicate with the Holy Spirit left me wondering whether I had ever been born again before. At least, this was like being born again for the second time, which is not really possible. Something exceptional had happened to me, far more wonderful than just having received healing. I had been changed in my innermost being. Gone was the tense, mind-controlling spirit which had been binding me for so long. I had lost my own grip upon myself and was instead being led by the Holy Spirit in a completely new way.

As a matter of fact, I could no longer work the way I used to. In the first months of my deliverance I tried to minister God's word according to the pattern I had always known, but it did not work out. I had always planned my messages well, figuring out a good time in advance what I would be speaking on and preparing the talk in great detail. Now I found myself standing before the congregation and speaking freely from my heart without paying attention to any written notes. The messages just flowed from my inner-most being as rivers of living waters.

For many this is perhaps no new thing, but for me, a systematic and analytical person with a logical and reasoning mind, this was nothing other than a revolution. I had never before in my twenty years of ministering God's word known such an anointing upon my spirit. Later, I realized that when the Lord visited me that morning and put His hand upon me, He had given me a much deeper trust and confidence in Himself. I was no longer tense, nervous or uptight when I was to deliver His word, and knew by a new spiritual intuition what to speak from His mind.

Now, one and a half years later, this is still the same. There is no way that I can go back to the old pattern, and why should I? This is so much better. It does not mean, however, that careful preparation in the study of God's word is not valid for me any more. Nor do I think that 'my way' has to be the way of anyone else. All I can say is that for me things have been so radically changed that I am a new man before God, with a much greater trust in my Lord and a very much increased confidence in the power and ability of the Holy Spirit.

God, by His graceful intervention, did not only bring me back to my former normal and good health. He took me a big step further in His eternal plan. I may be the same person, with the same temperament and the same sense of humour (only a lot worse now), but I have been changed in the most essential part of my being—in my spirit. The spirit has taken new control, where the mind and will previously dominated, and by God's mercy I have now learned more of what it is to walk in the Spirit.

It has taken a long time for me to work out in practice in my life all the words that were spoken to me by the Lord throughout the period in the dark tunnel, words that I could not comprehend at the time, but which came to life when the Lord spoke to me on my resurrection morning. I call His words 'lessons for a broken preacher', and as I continue to unfold in this book what the Lord revealed to me and what I learned through the years of pain, it is my prayer that my testimony of the Lord's goodness might be a help for other preachers in the furnace and also a warning to all of us to walk humbly before our God.

Chapter 8

A BROKEN SPIRIT

THE FIRST THING the Lord said was this:

> Johannes, all along this way you have been walking
> I have been longing to extend to you my healing touch, but
> I could not do it until you had been utterly broken before
> me. For in the days to come I cannot use you the way I
> have planned and give you my anointing in an increasing
> measure unless I know that your spirit is broken and your
> heart is contrite. I will not entrust my power and the heavy
> anointing of my Spirit to anyone who has not been broken.

I now began to understand the meaning of the best
known scripture, which had been with me all the way
through the dark tunnel, namely Psalm 23. I must have
quoted this psalm hundreds of times through the previous
three years. At the opening of this psalm the psalmist is
speaking about a wonderful time—how the Lord is allowing him to enjoy what I understand to be a real charismatic
experience, making him lie down in green pastures, leading
him beside the still waters and restoring his soul. Everything in this phase of his Christian experience seems to
testify to the fact that God has only happiness in store for
His children.

And then the picture suddenly changes radically. He
finds himself walking down a dark tunnel. There are no
green pastures any more and no quiet waters, only heavy
limitations and complete darkness. He calls it 'the valley of

the shadow of death'. It is as if everything is taken away from him, everything of that blessed overflowing sense of happiness, the wide and open field in the green pastures with plenty of food and the cool and refreshing waters. Down there in the long tunnel he discovers that when every outward success has been taken away from his life, the Lord is there with His rod and staff. He is comforted by nothing else but the cross. Only the Lord and nothing beside the Lord is there to lean on, to comfort him, to strengthen him and to lead him through.

Christ-confidence

The Lord seemed to indicate to me that He had allowed me to lose everything in order to lead me to that point, to the place where I could lean only on Him. He told me that He had to teach me from real experience that I could and should trust only in Him. For days of great darkness and difficulties would come, and only those who had a deep trust in the Lord would be able to stand. Now I had come to see from first-hand experience that I could never trust in any ability of my own and I could not trust in other people either. Only the Lord was trustworthy. He had shown me that when everything else failed, He did not fail, and He would be able to deliver to the utmost, yes, even from the dead.

Today I know that I can trust God, no matter what is in store in these last days. If He could bring me out from such a deep pit in thirty seconds, then there will never be another situation too difficult for Him to handle.

'Though I walk through the valley of the shadow of death, I will fear no evil, for you are with me; your rod and your staff, they comfort me.' His rod and His staff speak to me about His resurrection power, about the shepherd love and authority of the Lord Jesus, because of His finished work on the cross. We can suffer the loss of just about everything, but we can never lose His fellowship with us through the finished work of His cross. My testimony, like Paul's, is that:

> I am convinced that neither death nor life, neither angels nor demons, neither the present nor the future, nor any powers, neither height nor depth, nor anything else in all creation, will be able to separate us from the love of God that is in Christ Jesus our Lord (Rom 8:38–39).

That all-sufficient, glorious, eternal, finished work of the Lord Jesus on the cross shall cover us throughout life and for all eternity!

But there was more in Psalm 23 for me. The Lord pointed out that He could not anoint my head with the oil of the Spirit and let my cup flow over, or let me sit at His table in triumph over all my enemies unless He was sure that I had a broken spirit. In the days to come, when He will give of His anointing and power in measures that we have not known in earlier generations, it will be disastrous if our own self-will and self-life have not been crucified with Christ, if they have not been broken in real spiritual experience. All that power could eventually lead to a catastrophe if we have not come to walk humbly before God.

God cannot give us that enormous power of His if there is a risk of us becoming proud. The Lord told me that He had allowed me to be humiliated in front of practically all my friends all over the world by continuing to send me around in ministry and allowing many congregations to see my complete weakness and failure. When I broke down while ministering in Jersualem, and when I failed to fulfil my ministry and had to quit during a conference, it became clear to all that I was totally unable in my own person to serve the Lord.

> I did this to you, Johannes, in order for you to know, and all others to know, that if in the future you are used with power and blessing in your ministry, everybody will know that it was I, and only I, who worked through you.

These were the very words of the Lord that morning! He had to break my pride and make me realize that without Him I can do nothing, and that is final. Pride was the major problem. Not that I was aware of it. It was an attitude which crept in with the help of the Enemy.

After my experience in the tunnel, I simply cannot understand how people in the Christian world can talk about boosting your spiritual self-confidence, although I understand the intention, which is to try to help people overcome their inferiority complexes. I believe that not only the expression but also this whole approach is very wrong and unscriptural. We do not need more self-confidence because we are called not to boost our own selves, but to deny ourselves and put down our own life, to let it be crucified with Christ. The self-life has a curse upon it and is the centre of evil. It is the ally of the devil himself in his attempt to destroy us. We do not need more self-confidence. We need more Christ-confidence! That is why the message of the cross and of a broken spirit is so vital for the days of the great outpouring of God's Spirit.

If the devil cannot get us into plain sin of a grave moral sort, he will try to boost our pride in the spiritual gift we possess or in the 'success' of our ministry. This was his tactic with God's servant David. In both of David's big crises, pride was the underlying factor which led to his defeat. David's sin with Bathsheba had its root in the fact that David, knowing his enormous strength, no longer wanted to follow God's ruling that the king should always lead his army into battle. Instead, David let his generals, under the leadership of Joab, take control of the army of Israel, while he himself stayed back in his palace to relax and enjoy life. That sort of pride, of self-reliance, feeling himself so strong that he no longer had to obey God's rule, led to his tragic downfall. He came to realize that none of us can ever reach a point where we can be independent of the Lord. Self-reliance and self-confidence is pride, and pride turns God into our opponent instead of our close ally in the battle.

This pattern was even more clear in David's second big failure in his life as king of Israel. When his military strength was at its greatest, after he had subdued all his enemies, and the Enemy had no opportunity to get him in an open conflict, the devil put this thought into his mind: he should muster his army, just to see how strong he had in fact become. When he suggested the idea to Joab, the general immediately advised him against it, aware of the divine ordinance that did not allow any king of Israel to know his actual strength, lest he should be tempted to move independently of God. But David would not listen and demanded that the army be mustered, and so he brought the wrath of God upon his people. We know from the story how the angel of the Lord gave him three choices of calamity, and how he chose to fall into the hands of God. His big show of pride, however, cost the lives of 70,000 men of Israel (1 Chron 21).

God will not tolerate a spirit of pride in his chosen servants, and we cannot claim to be used by God if we are working in our own strength and through our own ambitions, because then the Lord will be against us. The divine law says that God opposes the proud, but gives grace to the humble. There can be times when we think that we are up against the Enemy, but it is in fact God who is fighting against us because our hearts are full of pride.

The ever-present Enemy

I know that people claim God will not withdraw His anointing from his servants even if they live an unclean life. Their gift can still operate, and people can still be both saved and healed by such ministries. Well, this claim must be qualified. It is true that God, being long-suffering with His people, seems to be willing to use His servants who are not living a holy life. But I believe that that will only be the case for a very limited period of time. If there is no repentance and brokenness, there is every danger of such ministers of God's word entering into apostasy, and if their gift is still working, it will be working more out of the influence of occult powers than of the power of the Holy Spirit.

We must never forget that the devil himself is very religious, and that he has the ability to perform signs and wonders. When Jesus in Matthew 7 speaks about some who claimed to have healed the sick, cast out demons and done signs and wonders in His name, but had never known the Lord, this is an instance of such a demonic takeover. They obviously started out in the Spirit, but went astray, fell away from the truth and ended up exercising their gift through occult power.

This is one reason why we should not focus completely on 'signs and wonders', but rather learn to follow the Lord and obey His commandments. We Christians are sometimes very funny people. The Lord ordered us to preach the word of truth, and then He would confirm it with signs following. And instead of doing just that we are getting so hooked on the signs and wonders that we forget to preach the gospel, and end up trying to produce that which is really only the by-product.

When the Lord explained Psalm 23 to me, I began to see that the precondition for living under this new anointing with oil and the overflowing cup of the Spirit was the experience of going down into the dark and lonesome tunnel. This was also the basis for enjoying God's peace, the kind of peace that would allow me to sit at His table and eat in the presence of enemies. First of all, that meant that in the future I would have to become used to the thought that enemies were present in my immediate circumstances, and that they would be watching me carefully, gathering around my table like dark vultures.

I dare say this is important to realize at a time when so many try to tell us that victorious Christian living is to fly high like a spiritual Batman, miles away from any kind of problem or difficulty. A type of need-orientated preaching seems to prevail in certain circles of the body of Christ, trying to make us believe that God has called us to use our spiritual power and gift to get rid of any obstacle we might possibly encounter. There are some Christians in this world whose only goal is to work themselves out of every pain or problem, using all their energy to remove everything unpleasant, because they have been told, falsely, that this is what people of faith do.

Alas, what kind of confusion is this? Does not the New Testament clearly teach us that we are called into battle and into an ongoing conflict, which will only end the minute Jesus puts His feet upon the Mount of Olives? We must get used to the idea of having the Enemy hanging around in everything we do and everywhere we go. It was easy for the psalmist to sit at God's table when he was in the green pastures, but in the very presence of all his enemies? Was the Lord not teaching me and everybody else that although the Enemy is strong and should not be underestimated, he is nevertheless a defeated foe and although he tries hard, he will not be able to overcome us? He certainly did try very hard in my life and in the life of my family, but in the end God proved that we who are in Christ are invincible.

So my tunnel experience gave me a whole new attitude towards the Enemy. I do not fear him any more. I know he is an awesome opponent, and I would not like to cause him to get any power over me again, but I also know that by God's grace he cannot beat me, he cannot kill me. Thanks to the finished work of the Lord Jesus, I can now have God's peace as I sit down to eat my spiritual food from God's table, knowing that the Enemy is watching me, but unable to hinder me from walking in the ways of the Lord. I know from experience how strong he can be, but I know something more: that my Lord is much stronger and holds the power over him. What a lesson!

Chapter 9

LET GOD BE GOD

W HEN GOD MET me in His power and grace I discovered that He did not leave me with the answers to all my questions. I also discovered that I no longer cared about getting answers to everything. The great deliverance from my past and the wonderful prospect for the future were enough. Meeting with God, seeing His glory, was all the answer I needed and desired.

The divine Controller

In the early months of my sickness, I remember how the Lord spoke a very strong word to my heart from Psalm 46:10: 'Be still, and know that I am God; I will be exalted among the nations, I will be exalted in the earth!' The remarkable thing about this word is the context in which it was spoken by God. Psalm 46 deals with a situation of extreme turmoil and upheaval in the land. The psalm speaks about mountains being shaken and waters being troubled, nations are raging and kingdoms falling. In such a crisis situation God does not speak about increased efforts and activities in order to protect oneself; He speaks about being still and coming to know Him as He is. And yet this is what is so difficult for us.

This was the real problem in my life. I had become so busy in God's business that the very things I was doing for the Lord hindered me from coming before the Lord and getting to know Him better. No wonder that I broke down in the end. Even spiritual business will prevent us from the most needed thing: sitting at the feet of the Lord to listen to His voice. The Lord Jesus warned us against being so weighed down by the cares of this life that we become spiritually dull and unable even to recognize the time when the Lord is about to come.

And yet it is so difficult for us to be clear about this problem of business, because we think that much we do for the Lord is justified in itself. There are people who believe that being involved in many activities is an expression of faith. I have come to the conclusion that it is more a sign of unbelief. We think that we have to carry the burdens and do the job, otherwise things will collapse around us and God will then be in trouble. Well, God must often have a big smile on His face as He considers all our important works, all our nervous and febrile activity.

The fact is that God is not at all affected by what is going on down here on earth. The shaking of mountains and nations would not affect Him, who sits on the throne, the slightest little bit. When God faces a great rebellion, such as that described in Psalm 2, when the kings and princes and rulers combined to cast off God's restraint, His response is none other than to laugh because his throne is for ever firm, and He has already installed His Anointed, His King upon His holy hill Zion. Jesus, the Son of God, has already been declared King of kings and Lord of lords and crowned as the only Ruler of the whole universe. God has everything under control. I remember a worship chorus that I learned many years ago in Sweden:

> He has everything in His hand,
> He has everything under control,
> and when I am praising Him
> I see who He really is.

We can trust this great God of ours and need not think that things are resting upon us.

The reason why it is so difficult for us to lay aside our work and be still and come to know God is that we are afraid of losing our positions or ministries, and that reveals our lack of trust in God, and reveals a spirit of unbelief. We must be there to help Him, to uphold His work.

Many years ago, Denis Clark, the founder of the prayer movement I serve, and a spiritual father to me, was speaking to a group of Christian leaders. I shall never forget what he said. 'When looking at the way so many of you pastors are "running" God's work, one can only come to the conclusion that you believe you in fact are God.' At first I felt most upset by this statement, being a pastor myself. Denis had a real gift of provoking his audience. After having given it much thought, I am beginning to believe that he is right. Many of God's servants responsible for churches or parachurch organizations behave as if they were minor kings, keeping everything in their domain under their tight control, allowing no one to move without their permission. It is not difficult for me to recognize myself in this picture from my earlier years in the ministry.

The question is, who is the Head of the church or the work? Haven't we sometimes occupied that place which belongs solely to the only head of the church, the Lord Jesus? If so, no wonder we get overbusy, and no wonder we end up burned out or broken down! Would any of us really want to be God and carry the load of responsibility for all God's creation? We are not God, and thank God for that. We are not even gods, as some modern-day heretics are trying to tell us. We are just human beings honoured by God's grace to stand in His house and serve Him. What a release it is to realize that God is God, and we can trust Him and need not rely on our own activities. So many pastors, evangelists and even whole churches are under heavy stress because they have taken into their own hands things which only God can do.

Beyond understanding

It is wonderful to meet men and women of God who really know Him. Their lives radiate rest and confidence, even if they normally have much to do. They do not rely on their own understanding. In days when the servants of God must have all the answers, it is most blessed to meet people who know God well enough to realize that only God has the answers. The greatest men of God I have met were those who dared to meet some of my questions with a clear, 'I don't know'!

How different has been my experience with those who believe they are 'gods'. I met a young minister of God's word who tried to tell me that he was never in doubt over any spiritual thing, and that his healing gift had so far worked 100 per cent—nobody he had prayed for had left unhealed. Well, I became the first one, and of course there were dozens of others like me. I know that for a fact. Yet he thought that his statement expressed 'faith', not knowing that he was lying and was suffering from his own foolishness and spiritual immaturity. Haven't we all come across the words of St Paul: 'The man who thinks he knows something does not yet know as he ought to know' (1 Cor 8:2)! It is far better to know God than to know everything.

When Job was suffering, he did not know why. He could not find an answer. Only his three so-called friends knew everything and added to his pain and sorrow by their foolishness. If one has friends like Job's it is hardly necessary to have any enemies. As Job went on, bewildered, in his suffering they came up with the simplest logical answers. He had committed some secret sin and God was now punishing him for it. All he needed was to repent of that unknown sin and everything would be all right. How wrong they were. Job knew God well enough not to believe that God would punish him for something he had done unwittingly, and so he would not accept the answers of his friends. He also knew that God has the right to do things in our lives which we do not understand. So the discussion went on.

Ground down by his theological friends, who knew everything about how things work in life and how God is supposed to function, in the end Job became somewhat infected by these ideas, so that he himself began to question God's dealings and to argue with the Almighty. This is when the Lord made an unusual suggestion, namely that He should act the role of a student and Job should then assume the role of His theological tutor, telling Him how He should act and function in His relationship with His creation. But Job realizes that this is a bad idea, and immediately suggests that it should be the other way round: God should be the teacher, and he, Job, would listen humbly to God's lesson. And then God gives His servant a lesson in zoology, beginning by describing the life and nature of a crocodile. God points out to Job how this monster of an animal crushes everyone who comes in its way; it is violent and lawless. In the middle of His lesson the Lord comes to the main point: this terrible creature, which does no good, and does not seem to fulfil any useful purpose, has been designed and created by God Himself! Then Job realizes his great mistake: he had tried to limit God, to fit Him into the frame of the human mind! And Job throws himself down before God and utters these words:

> I know that you can do all things; no plan of yours can be thwarted. You asked, 'Who is this that obscures my counsel without knowledge?' Surely I spoke of things I did not understand, things too wonderful for me to know. You said, 'Listen now, and I will speak; I will question you, and you shall answer me.' My ears had heard of you but now my eyes have seen you. Therefore I despise myself and repent in dust and ashes (Job 42:2–6).

Job had tried to limit God to that which can be understood by the human mind, and had not allowed God to go beyond the boundaries. That is really the same as trying to make God in our image instead of realizing that we are made in His image. The curse of humanism in Christian theology reduces God to the level of a human being, which in fact means that He is no longer God. If God can function only within the bounds of human understanding, He is no longer God, but a man like the rest of us. This is the tragic result of much so-called theology today: God is being deprived of His divine and supernatural Being, and He is no longer allowed to move outside of the human intellect.

Let me ask you a question: Can God do things in your life beyond what you have so far experienced, and beyond your present theology? If not, you are going to be in deep trouble one of these days, because in the last days God will act in history and in the lives of His people in ways that are beyond understanding!

It has been my experience over the last few years that God has systematically destroyed my theology. I remember how, at the beginning of the spiritual renewal, I heard that some Lutherans had been baptized in the Holy Spirit and were actually speaking in new tongues. I simply could not believe it. Speaking in tongues was only for us Pentecostals, and besides, these Lutherans had the wrong kind of water baptism! How could God meet with such people and bless them with the gift of His Spirit? And then I had to bow to the fact that these Lutherans, whom I knew personally, really were baptized with the Spirit. It was some time before I could take that in, but it became a whole lot worse when later I heard that even some Catholics had received the power of God's Spirit. This was just too much. As a genuine Pentecostal I had always believed that Catholics were not real Christians and that the Pope was the Anti-christ himself, so I had to believe that this was more from the devil than from God. But I was proven quite wrong, and some of the most devoted Spirit filled people I know of today are charismatic Catholics. God had moved far beyond my spiritual understanding and done so without asking me!

If only we could let God be God and honour Him as the great and sovereign God, whose heart and mind is so much greater than ours. Did not the Lord, through the prophet

Isaiah, say to His people that His ways and His thoughts are as much higher than ours as the heavens are higher than the earth? Do we think that we have figured out God? Or can He still in His infinite Being surprise us limited human beings? Job never received any answers as to why he had to suffer so much. At least, the Scripture does not tell us so. I did not get any direct answer to why I had to spend time down in the tunnel, but through it all I came face to face with the King Himself, and like Job I am able to say today 'My ears had heard of you but now my eyes have seen you' (Job 42:5)! There are many things we will never have an answer to on this side of eternity, and God will not give us these answers partly because we do not have His capacity to understand things and partly because knowing too much would lead us away from knowing God as One who is so much greater and wiser than we are.

Chapter 10

STRENGTHEN YOUR BROTHERS

I F ANY ONE biblical character can illustrate the type of crisis I went through, it is most certainly Simon Peter. Of course, I would never dare to compare myself with this tremendous servant of God in any other way. Neither can I say that I denied the Lord in the same way as he did, but his experience of failure, defeat, brokenness and final restoration is very much like mine.

Sifted as wheat

Anyway, the words which the Lord Jesus spoke to this the chief among the disciples were given to me directly by the Lord not only during my trial, but also on the morning of the healing miracle:

> Simon, Simon, Satan has asked to sift you as wheat. But I have prayed for you, Simon, that your faith may not fail. And when you have turned back, strengthen your brothers (Lk 22:31–32).

The Lord could not see any other way to break that spirit of self-reliance and self-confidence in Peter's heart than to allow him to go through this horrible experience, because an unbroken servant is useless to the Lord. When we are stubborn and not willing to yield to the cross, God has no other alternative but to let us fall into the hands of the

Enemy. Satan is constantly demanding that God should let him have a go at us. He is the Accuser of the brethren, accusing them day and night before God.

Ongoing rebellion and hardness of heart will eventually cause God to give in to the demands of the devil, and so will unrepented sin of any kind. God has no choice, because the Creator of the universe must bow to the rules and moral laws He Himself has laid down. Sin and rebellion and pride give Satan power in the lives of individuals as well as in creation. Satan rules only where sin is being held onto and God's grace and forgiveness is being rejected. God had to let the demand of Satan be carried out, that Peter be sifted as wheat.

I have to say very clearly here that a substantial part of my sufferings was caused by my own disobedience, so in that respect I can relate to Peter, but not to Job, who I believe suffered only for the sake of God's purposes. However, based on the Lord's words to me that morning, I can also say that part of my affliction was to prepare and equip me for service, to give me something whereby I would be able to strengthen my brethren.

That element was certainly also evident in Peter's crisis. The expression 'to sift you as wheat' is much more positive than it sounds. The Lord was pointing to the fact that Satan, in his attempt to destroy Peter, would not be allowed to go too far because God had set a limit. In the end the temptations and the suffering inflicted upon God's servant would turn out to serve God's interests. Isn't that a most encouraging thought! In the case of Job, you will remember that the Lord also drew the line for Satan's activity: he would be allowed to touch Job's possessions, his health and his family, but not to take his life. God set a limit for the Enemy, which proves to us that our God is indeed sovereign, and that the Enemy cannot move beyond what God in His purposes allows him to do.

That does not eliminate the danger of the Enemy's attack, and we should never come to 'sleep' on any pillow of 'eternal safety'. Although God sets a limit, our reaction and response to the whole situation are nevertheless crucial because if the devil cannot take our lives, which is what he always wants to do, there is still the possibility that we could do so ourselves, pressurized by the pain and horror. Job's most critical moment, I believe, was when his wife put a most tempting suggestion to him: 'Curse God and die!' The aim of the devil is always for us to leave the Lord, to turn our back on God, to depart from our faith in Him. Thank God, Job did not pay attention to his wife in that respect, but kept fearing God more than anything else.

What really was the deeper purpose in Peter's trial? It was that the chaff of his life should be separated from the wheat! The sifting process does just that. When, in the old days, they sifted they had no machine to help them but would spread the wheat on the ground and let the oxen trample right over it until the chaff was torn off. Then, with big forks, they would toss the wheat in the air so that the wind would blow away the light chaff, and the heavy part, the grains of wheat, would fall to the ground. The result was a total separation of the two elements. This was the outcome of Peter's trial. This painful crisis broke his pride and reliance on his own power. When he later encountered the Lord in deep repentance, the chaff of his own pride had gone and left was the precious grain of faith in his heart.

The devil got nothing out of his furious assault. Instead, he helped God cleanse and purify His servant. Notice that when the Lord announced Peter's affliction, He did not pray that he would be prevented from falling into the hands of Satan, but that as he was delivered into the power of the Enemy, his faith would not fail. It is clear that the object of the Lord's praying was to deliver Peter from himself and strengthen his faith. Is this not a biblical principle, found over and over again in the Scriptures? The apostle Peter himself frequently refers to this matter in his letters.

Listen to this:

> In this you greatly rejoice, though now for a little while you may have had to suffer grief in all kinds of trials.

These have come so that your faith—of greater worth than gold, which perishes even though refined by fire—may be proved genuine and may result in praise, glory and honour when Jesus Christ is revealed (1 Pet 1:6-7).

This was also the testimony of Job:

But he knows the way that I take; when he has tested me, I shall come forth as gold (Job 23:10).

To those who deny the place of trials and suffering in the Christian life I can only say that you are not only way off the mark in matters of truth, but you are depriving God's people of spiritual growth and strength! No matter how much you try to boost your faith, you will never be able to get hold of God's faith unless you are willing to accept the discipline of the Holy Spirit in your life.

To God be the glory

The chief purpose of any trial, of course, is to bring glory to the name of Jesus. Now I am in a most fortunate position in that regard. I cannot brag about anything in me, but I am able to glorify the name of Jesus in a way I have never been able to before. This is the real aim of my testimony, to manifest the power and the glory of the Lord Jesus, my Lord and my Messiah. God's greatest motive in bringing me through that burning furnace was that I would become a living proof of His grace and power, so that His name might be praised and worshipped wherever I go and tell my story.

During the first year of my healing I have not missed one opportunity to tell about His love and power. Now and again some have objected to that for reasons I have never really been able to figure out. But I cannot help that. On the morning of 25th February 1989 the Lord specifically asked me to let my experience bring glory to His name in all the places where I had formerly exposed my weakness and failure. I intend to be faithful to that request by the Lord.

That is also the reason why I have written this book. I want as many people as possible to see the glory of God and to be encouraged to follow Him and to trust Him in a deeper way.

But there is another side to the question of why God took me through these deep waters. He wanted to provide me with a testimony that could strengthen my brothers, just as he told Peter, 'And when you have turned back, strengthen your brothers.' I am now in a position to give 'live' proof of God's resurrection power. I can not only speak about it, I am living proof of His love and power!

This was how Paul understood his trials.

> Praise be to the God and Father of our Lord Jesus Christ, the Father of compassion and the God of all comfort, who comforts us in all our troubles, so that we can comfort those in any trouble with the comfort we ourselves have received from God. For just as the sufferings of Christ flow over into our lives, so also through Christ our comfort overflows. If we are distressed, it is for your comfort and salvation; if we are comforted, it is for your comfort, which produces in you patient endurance of the same sufferings we suffer (2 Cor 1:3–6).

It is quite clear from this that God has a purpose in our trials—to enable us to minister to the members of the body of Christ.

For a start, the very fact that a man like me, who used to radiate security and faith, could become a victim of pain, doubt and depression, has, in a strange way, helped others who thought that they were especially weak and hopeless and that spiritual 'supermen' were more supernatural than human. Over and over again I have heard people say they have been comforted by seeing that a well known servant of God is just as weak and human as they are. It has helped them to get away from the thought that they were con-demned and rejected. There is comfort in knowing that you are not alone and that it is not totally abnormal to be faced with problems, suffering and sickness. We are all weak and made of clay, dust of the earth under the corruption of the Fall. No one is safe from its effects and no one is yet without flaws and weaknesses, perfect and holy. We all have to go through suffering in this life. All other talk is nonsense and unreal.

Another thing which has brought comfort to many people is the fact that a man can reach a point where his condition seems absolutely impossible and hopeless, and yet be renewed, even when he has no faith left, and all the good advice and therapies have had no effect upon him and he has been given up by all, and he himself has given up. Yet God does not give up, but comes in at the last hour and makes everything whole. Many depressed people have found new hope and expectation by realizing that it is still possible for deeply depressed and mentally disturbed people to experience deliverance and healing; also, that God has the last word and that the devil is not able to go further than God allows. God has set a limit, and when we do not know where we are or what to do, God is still in control. I have heard many brothers and sisters express their gratitude for the fact that God is moving in His own time, and if we decide to be patient and not force the situation by human power, He will come, sometimes fairly late, but never too late!

It has also been a tremendous comfort for some deeply afflicted children of God to understand, through my trial, that God is dealing with us in His love, that there is a purpose to our affliction, that it will lead to personal strength and growth, to being molded and changed into the likeness of Jesus, and later being able to help and minister to other sick members of the body of Jesus.

In this connection, people have also been immensely encouraged to realize that they do not need to come up with a straight answer to what they are going through, and that they will possibly never get an answer to their situation or that of others until we all stand before the Lord in glory. But God is able to give them His peace which surpasses all understanding, and guard their thoughts and hearts in Christ, whether they are able to find answers or not.

But above all this, the great encouragement is that God's miracles are not out of date, that He is still performing His supernatural acts in the nineties of what is perhaps the last century of our age, that nothing is impossible with God, and that a healing process does not have to take a long time. The fact that God once again has proved that He is the 'God, who raises the dead' has comforted and strengthened the brethren all over the world. The time for God's supernatural workings is not over. Indeed, I believe we are in the last period of time in the history of the church, when the 'acts of the apostles' will become a daily occurrence in the lives of God's people.

It has been a joy for me to have been able to pray for depressed people everywhere in my ministry, and to the glory of God I can say that quite a few have received real help and a few even instant deliverance, and of course I now have a special place in my heart for people in that category. That is part of God's eternal purpose for my life.

One last thing. The outcome of my crisis has produced much comfort and encouragement in the area of prayer. People have seen that prayer is rewarding, and that in the long run God will honour even the smallest and most feeble prayer from His children. Those who have prayed for someone over a long period of time have been renewed and refreshed in their intercession, realizing that they have not wasted their time, and that in God's appointed hour mighty results will come out of their faithful prayer ministry. Just as it has been truly said that we cannot outgive God, it can be even more truly said that nobody can outpray Him. He remains the faithful Rewarder of those who seek Him!

Chapter 11

YOUNG AGAIN LIKE THE EAGLE

THERE ARE STILL two more scriptures which the Lord commented on as I listened to Him on that wonderful resurrection morning.

The Potter and the clay

He reminded me of a word that, together with Psalm 46:10, was the very first word that entered my mind when I realized that I was sick. A full picture of the potter and his clay, as recorded in Jeremiah chapter 18, was painted, so to speak, on my mind. The Lord let me understand that the first vessel had failed to become what the great Potter had intended it to be, not because of any lack of skill in the hands of the Potter, but because of the bad quality of the clay and its stubborn resistance to be formed according to the divine will.

How amazing it is, though, that the great Potter does not reject the bad clay and throw it out as dung. A modern-day potter would have done that and started afresh with new and better clay because clay has never been expensive. But instead of throwing out the worthless clay, the great Potter decides to deal with the clay in order to make it more smooth and pliable and malleable. The Lord told me that the three years of trouble had served that purpose. He had broken me through the circumstances of physical and mental weakness and given me a broken spirit and a contrite heart so that He could mould me all over again into a vessel after His own design.

The remarkable thing about this parable in Jeremiah 18 is that in His second attempt the Lord does not think about shaping the vessel according to the original design, but now makes it to a new one. The Lord made it clear to me that after what I had been going through, I should not return to the old pattern of things. He had something else, something new for me, a reshaping of my life and ministry based on His divine observations of my character and my temperament. His purpose for my future ministry was that there would be areas where I would no longer move as before, and other new areas where I would move in. In all of this I would have to follow the Lord's lead very carefully. Such were His words to me. I was a new vessel, shaped and formed to be able to serve God's purposes.

God's eternal plans

I remember how this word became very practical. Having laid down my previous work and positions, I had to seek the Lord after my healing and ask him: What now? What should I be doing and where should I go? Of course, I had imagined that God's answer to these questions would be a systematic plan and schedule for the next couple of years, but not so. I was in a new place, where I would no longer need the old system. All the Lord said to me was simply the words from Ephesians 2:10: 'For we are God's workmanship, created in Christ Jesus to do good works, which God prepared in advance for us to do.' There was no need to worry about the future work, and there was no need for me to try to do my own planning. God already had a well prepared and detailed plan with specific works, and all I needed was to discover that planned way and walk in it.

Really, this is fantastic when you think about it. The original Greek for 'in advance' does not just mean last week or even last year, but from the foundation of the world. God is not at all confused as to what He would like us to do for Him and He has no last minute calls or assignments. The plans have been prepared from the beginning of time, and we can rest calmly in His hands just trying to discover what the Spirit of God is saying and what He is leading us to do.

Following the words from Ephesians, the Lord pointed out a few things as guidelines for my future ministry. I was not to go back to my seven leadership responsibilities again. I was no longer to stay in a position of leadership in the local church. The Lord would give me only one ministry responsibility for the time being, and that was to give myself full time to co-ordinate International Intercessors. I was no longer allowed to work on my own, but was to team up with others in the same ministry.

When I later asked the Lord with whom I was supposed to team up for the future ministry in Intercessors International, He let me see, as on a television screen, our good and close friends Barbara and Berthold Becker from Intercessors for Germany. In a vision they appeared hand in hand, smiling at me, but they did not say anything. From this I concluded that the Lord had called Erna, my wife, and me to join together with Barbara and Berthold. And that is what happened. Today we are living in the south of Germany, sharing an office with Berthold and feeling very well and very happy. Yet another of God's miracles is the way in which we were able, without money, to make such a major move to another nation. All we can say is that the Lord's word has come true, every bit of it, and we give Him all the glory.

'Wait on the Lord'

When I was walking in the wilderness of desolation, more than once the word from Isaiah 40:30–31 had been ringing in my ears:

> Even the youths shall faint and be weary, and the young
> men will utterly fall, but those who wait on the Lord shall

renew their strength; they shall mount up with wings like
eagles, they shall run and not be weary, they shall walk
and not faint (Is 40:30–31, NKJV).

I could certainly identify myself with the young men who
fainted and became weary, although they were in the prime
of life and at the peak of their natural strength. I had
become burned out at a pretty young age.

One friend told me that before my breakdown I had
looked unusually young for my age, but after I was hit with
this darkness I looked, moved and behaved like an eighty-
year-old man. Well, I had experienced that the natural
resources of even a younger man can easily be exhausted
when he goes on in his own power. I had not been running
on God's energy any more, walking in the Spirit, who is
inexhaustible in His eternal life and power.

It is said in the same chapter of Isaiah that God, the
everlasting God, the Lord, the Creator of the ends of the
earth neither faints nor is weary and His understanding is
unsearchable. And then the good news follows: those who
wait upon the Lord shall renew their strength and mount up
like eagles. Here the Scripture, as in so many other places,
is comparing the spiritual life with the life and nature of the
eagle, and in the life of the eagle a most unusual change
occurs. After the first couple of years an eagle loses the
white flying feathers which enable it to soar, and has to sit
in the cleft of a rock for quite some time until the new blue
flying feathers of a grown-up eagle have grown to their full
length, then it can throw itself out over the rock and fly
high, higher than ever before.

The time of waiting is not at all pleasant for this active
bird of prey. Completely cut off from its normal life it has
to sit and wait and watch its fellow eagles soaring in the
sunshine. Once the 'waiting' eagle is ready to fly again we
can speak of it 'being young again', having its second youth.
From this one can speak of one's youth being renewed like
the eagle's, a phrase found in that wonderful psalm of
redemption, Psalm 103:

Praise the Lord, O my soul,
and forget not all his benefits.
He forgives all my sins
and heals all my diseases;
he redeems my life from the pit
and crowns me with love and compassion.
He satisfies my desires with good things,
so that my youth is renewed like the eagle's (Ps 103:2–5).

This is exactly what happened to me. People around me tell me that I look younger and more alive than before my trial, and certainly in my heart and spirit I feel completely renewed. By the grace of God I have received my 'second youth', maybe not so much in the natural life, but certainly in the spiritual. I have never felt better, and by God's mercy I have never been stronger than I am now. This is a new phase in my life. I am experiencing a new freedom in the Spirit to soar high up in the heavenlies. Life has become new to me, and I can only say that these new 'blue feathers' of the fully grown eagle are much better than the 'white feathers' of childhood. Living and serving God in this 'second vessel' is far better than in the first one that broke to pieces. This is what I understand to be 'spiritual renewal'!

God promises this kind of renewal to all of His children, provided they know what it is to wait on Him. 'Those who wait on the Lord shall renew their strength; they shall mount up with wings like eagles'! This vital spiritual truth of 'waiting on the Lord' has been pushed back by all the 'action doctrines' that have flooded the body of Christ in our day, and that is probably one of the main reasons why so many brothers and sisters are weary and burned out.

I have to admit, though, that waiting is hard for people who, like me, are impatient, but it is nevertheless a most rewarding quality in the kingdom of God. In Denmark we have an old saying: If you wait long enough, you may become the king of Sweden! Well, I don't know about that. These days you would have to wait a very long time because Sweden has a young king. But there is a lot of truth in the saying anyway, both in ordinary life as well as in the spiritual life. I recall how the way David became the king of Israel impressed me. He had to wait for twenty years from the moment he was appointed until the day when he could actually reign as king over Israel. Waiting became a lifestyle for David. He had to learn to move in God's time for everything he had been promised. With Saul it was quite different. He was made king almost instantly, and an impulsive and impatient spirit was a major flaw in his character, which eventually cost him the crown.

God's servant Moses was another one who had to learn to wait on the Lord. His impulsive nature led to forty years in the wilderness, where he came to realize that God's work of delivering His people had to be carried out in His appointed time.

Even the Son of God had to wait. It is incredible to think that for the first thirty years of His life Jesus lived as just an ordinary carpenter, until God's appointed hour had come for His public ministry to begin.

One thing that bothers me today is the teaching that we can have everything from God in our experience here and now. The fact that we are born again, filled with the Spirit and have Christ dwelling in us means that we are perfect and can handle the whole heritage any time we want. This is nothing less than false teaching, and it is very dangerous and harmful to God's people because it creates so many illusions and leaves many Christians deeply discouraged and depressed when they discover after a while, that it does not work that way at all.

This teaching leads people to act like the prodigal son. He was the heir of his rich father and if he had waited he could have been very happy. Instead, he insisted on having his inheritance paid out in ready cash, not knowing that he was far too immature to handle that kind of money. And what happened? He destroyed himself and ended up in deep misery and disgrace. Well, thank God for his loving father, who later forgave him and restored him as he finally decided to turn back to the father's house.

Friends, we are not meant to be deluged with everything that God has for us in this short span of time. God's goodness and riches are so great that it will take eternity to exhaust everything He has prepared for us in His love. Our lives as His children must never be seen as a few years or even a lifetime; they must be seen in the light of eternity. And that is why we have to learn to wait on the Lord. As a little chorus says, 'God does everything He wants in His time.'

It is those who wait on the Lord who shall renew their strength and mount up like eagles, while others, even the young and powerful, who do not know this secret will grow weary and faint.

Chapter 12

A MOVEMENT OF GRACE

ALL ALONG, AS I have been writing this book, I have never been in doubt as to how I should end this story. Everything I experienced from God during this most dramatic period of my life can be summed up in one word: *grace!*

No matter how I look at it, I come to that same conclusion: God has manifested Himself as the God of grace! This word 'grace' is explained as 'the undeserved favour of God'. The greatest truth of the whole Bible is, of course, that God has granted us human beings, us sinners, His most 'undeserved favour'.

It has always been a deep desire of my heart that I might come to know the ways of God, the way in which God is dealing with His people. A long time ago I was made aware of the well known statement that God let Moses see His ways, whereas the children of Israel could only see His deeds. How we need to appreciate that today when so many of God's people focus on signs and wonders and other mighty deeds. We need to understand why God is doing what He is doing. In other words, we need to come to know God's ways. But that is not easy because the Scripture clearly states that 'His ways [are] past finding out' (AV)! So are we not asking something impossible? Well, I understand God's ways to be past figuring out when it comes to the human mind and intellect, for elsewhere Paul speaks about us having God's Spirit and being able to have God's mind about things. So I believe that I can come to know God's ways as long as I am seeking to understand them in the Spirit.

God's ways are, of course, quite different from our ways. They are of another realm, so to speak. We are earthly. He is heavenly. That is why the Bible points out that the ways of God are as high above ours as heaven is high above the earth. Therefore, in coming to know something about God's ways we must be prepared for great surprises.

One thing that is extraordinary is found in Romans 5:20, a verse dealing with grace: 'The law was added so that the trespass might increase. But where sin increased, grace increased all the more.'

First of all, this tells us that God enforced His law upon mankind and thus increased the problem of sin. That means that trying to live according to the law will only lead to sin. For this reason legalism in the church—activity outside of God's Spirit—is such a deadly thing and causes nothing but misery and unhappiness. You will never be able to improve your life by your own efforts. The law causes only an increase of sin. God deals effectively with the problem of sin in another way: 'Where sin increased, grace increased all the more'!

In other words, God did not focus on any negative effort to remove the sin in the world. We would most certainly have done that. Every time we discover that something is out of order, we immediately start to try to rectify it, correct it or repair it. We human beings, and this goes for many believers too, focus so much on the problems that we never discover the solutions. I have found that thousands of Christians, including pastors and whole churches, are so engaged in working on the problems of individuals, churches and even society, that they miss the whole point and never get anywhere.

Instead of fighting the negative power of sin directly, God decided to go another way—to provide something positive and far more powerful and send it into the world. And it is by receiving the good news in the midst of the bad that we find the measure and the power of grace is superseding the power of sin. In one way God does not seem to bother much about the presence of sin in the world because He knows that He has let loose a power which is much more powerful.

Light in the darkness

God's answer to sin was that 'when the time had fully come, God sent his Son, born of a woman, born under law'. 'When the time had fully come' does not mean the most convenient moment in history according to human understanding. On the contrary, it was the darkest hour of history, when everything was hopeless and the world was dominated by the pagan Roman Empire. Into this situation God sent His answer, a child born in a stable, the Lord and Messiah Jesus Christ, our Saviour.

Speaking of light and darkness, how do you think we can get rid of darkness in any given place? A friend of mine once experimented in a church where he was preaching about light and darkness. He got the permission of the pastor and the elders to turn off the electric light in the church so that everyone was sitting in complete darkness. He then asked the pastor and the elders to open all the doors and windows in the church and form a line and begin to push the darkness out of the building. Of course, they all laughed at his suggestion, realizing what we all know, that this cannot be done this way. And when the evangelist asked how to solve the problem and get the darkness out of the church, everybody agreed that there was only one way: to switch on the light! An African proverb expresses this truth by saying, 'It is better to light a candle than to start cursing the darkness!' That is God's way. He sent the light in the midst of the darkness and, as the apostle John puts it, 'the darkness has not overcome it' (Jn 1:5, RSV).

How should we then deal with this problem of the sinful nature? Not by focusing on sin, not by working to get rid of it, but by receiving the grace which has been so abundantly provided by God. Our basic problem is not so much how to get rid of something as how to receive something, and that which we receive, God's grace, will push away the works of sin. Did not Paul tell us that the way to be victorious over the flesh is to walk in the Spirit? Listen to these words: 'For if you live according to the sinful nature, you will die; but if by the Spirit you put to death the misdeeds of the body, you will live' (Rom 8:13).

Walking in the Spirit finishes off the flesh altogether. What we need is more of the Spirit, lives more filled with the Spirit, then we will deliver a devastating blow to the power of sin in our lives. More grace leads to less sin. Is this not good news? Turn away from yourself. Stop working so much on your problems and receive from God His powerful grace!

The principle of grace applies even to the world situation. You remember that the Lord, when speaking about the last days, told a parable about a man having sown wheat in his field. Later on his servants discovered that not only wheat was growing in the field but also a lot of tares. Naturally they suggested to their master that they go out in the field and cut down the tares. But the master said no. He was afraid that cutting down the tares could harm his wheat, and he ordered them to wait until harvest time. Jesus used this to illustrate the way God is working, and as I have already pointed out, God does not seem to be eager to remove evil and sin from the world. He has appointed a day in history, at the very end of time, when He will deal with the tares and burn them. But until the day when the Lord comes, I am afraid the problem of sin is going to be even worse. Should we then use our energy to try to prevent sin? Or could it be a better investment of our time and energy to spread the good news of God's unlimited grace in the world?

God's way of overcoming evil is certainly revolutionary. Paul said this when telling us how we should handle our enemies:

If your enemy is hungry, feed him; if he is thirsty, give him something to drink. In doing this, you will heap burning coals on his head. Do not be overcome by evil but overcome evil with good (Rom 12:20–21).

I am in no way suggesting that we should not fight against evil when it comes to demonic principalities and powers. I am doing that most of the time as I am engaged in prayer and spiritual warfare. These verses tell us we should not fight against people according to the principle of the law, but by God's way of grace, and knock them out by showing them the love of Jesus. Again the positive power of God's love is far greater than all the evils of this world.

May I also suggest from my reading of 1 Corinthians that unity in the body of Christ comes into being to a greater extent when God's people stop correcting one another's faults and start to receive a fuller measure of God's Holy Spirit? When we live in the Spirit we will be able to overcome that which separates us from one another in the body of Jesus. Division is almost always a result of the activity of the carnal nature.

And how about evangelizing people? We live in a time when evangelism has become a major activity of the church, and rightly so. But in our eagerness to win the world for Christ we sometimes follow modern business principles rather than God's way. I have had the privilege of participating in some of the major consultations on world evangelism, and although I appreciate every effort being made to spread the gospel around the globe, I must admit that I do not believe in some of the methods adopted by evangelistic organizations. The use of modern technology—radio, and television and computers—does not convince me. I have nothing against the use of these and other modern tools, but I simply cannot put my trust in them. When Jesus gave His disciples the great commission, He did not say, 'And when the computers come on you, then you shall be my witness until the end of the world.' He did say, 'When the Holy Spirit comes on you', and that I believe in. Our trust must not be in anything we can accomplish, but in the ability and the power of God's Holy Spirit. People in the world need to find grace, not to be confronted with tons of paper or programmes. Paul pointed out that it would be 'the kindness of God' that would lead people to repentance (Rom 2:4).

How are we approaching people with the gospel? Are we using God's way? How did the Lord Jesus lead people to come to believe in Him? The story of the woman He met at the well is most revealing (Jn 4:4–30). The Lord did not begin by pointing out the many sins for which she could expect God's punishment and eternal condemnation. He approached her with grace, putting before her God's gift of living water which would enable her to never thirst again. And she wanted that water badly. Then the Lord told her that for her to receive the gift of God she needed to put certain things in order and repent of certain sins. At that point her heart so desired the Lord's gift that she was willing to do anything to get it! This is God's way of grace. Friends, we scarcely need to point out people's sins to them—they know them very well themselves. What we need is to be able somehow to become channels of that grace, which is far more abundant than sin.

Triumphing over troubles

Grace ultimately triumphs over our Enemy. It enables God to turn into good everything that was meant for evil, and make it work for our eternal benefit. Through my crisis I have gained a clearer perspective on the circumstances of life and even the activities of the devil. God's grace is unique and it can make everything in our lives positive and fruitful.

Was this not the experience of the great apostle Paul, even when he suffered horrific opposition, troubles and riots against him. And in addition he had a strange thorn in his flesh: a messenger of darkness permitted by God to hinder him. Although he prayed for it to be removed, the answer of God was no. Or to put it like this: God's way was different. God said that He would not remove Paul's persecution and troubles, but He would give him sufficient grace. 'My grace,' said the Lord, 'is sufficient for you, for my power is made perfect in weakness' (2 Cor 12:9). God did not change Paul's circumstances, but He used them to let His triumphant grace prevail. These difficulties produced much glory for God and promoted His kingdom because of the grace poured out in ever increasing measures in Paul's life. In the end, the messenger of hell who bothered Paul would have regretted his actions as he discovered that he had been the instrument in producing the grace through which Paul led thousands of people to the Lord.

Often, when we talk about 'overcoming', we do so in connection with being delivered from troubles and pain. It is questionable whether that has anything at all to do with the biblical concept of overcoming. At least, if so, it is a very low and selfish level of triumph.

My good friend Steve Lightle pointed out once, on a ministry tour in Israel, that there are two levels of overcoming, as seen in the two different encounters the Lord Jesus had with the stormy Sea of Galilee. One time when He was in the boat with his disciples a terrible storm blew up, and the Lord, in response to the pleas of his frightened disciples, stood up and calmed the sea completely by His divine authority. But the next time, the disciples are alone in their boat, fighting off the storm. Suddenly they see the Lord walking on the sea. He does not bother about calming the sea, but shows that we can reach a point in our life with God where we can triumph over life's storms and troubles, not exempted from them but right in the middle of them.

Paul wrote these remarkable words: 'In [not outside] all these things we are more than conquerors through him who loved us' (Rom 8:37). He was not speaking about a Sunday school picnic, but trouble, hardship, persecution, famine, nakedness, danger, the sword'. In all this, he said, we will triumph, not by our own glory and strength, but by the grace of our Lord Jesus!

Despite experiencing such a dramatic miracle of healing in my life, I still have problems, and the Enemy still has a go at me. Circumstances are much the same as previously, but I am not the same. By God's grace I seem to be able to cope with situations better, to overcome whatever I am being confronted with.

Also, although I was miraculously healed in spirit, soul and body, I am still left with a physical weakness in my heart. Now and again my heart loses its normal perfect rhythm, and I still have to take drugs to prevent further attacks. This condition is no problem as such, and even has its advantages.

First of all, it is a small but effective warning signal, reminding me never to overdo things again and to allow myself to have proper times of rest. The life I lead involves much travel, and I need such a warning.

But the major benefit of this minor handicap is that I am constantly reminded of God's great goodness and grace throughout my recent period of suffering. It makes me think of God's servant Jacob who limped after wrestling with the angel of the Lord—a reminder of the struggle and victory that changed him from Jacob, the worm, into Israel, a prince of God. And as he came to the last hours of his life and spoke his final words of blessing over his twelve sons, the Scripture says that 'Jacob, when he was dying... worshipped as he leaned on the top of his staff' (Heb 11:21). At the very end of his life Jacob was able to worship God and give Him thanks for that painful, dramatic event which had crushed his thigh and left him crippled for the rest of his life, but which had brought immense blessings from God into his life and that of his family and made him one of the most effective servants of the living God.

As long as I live and until I stand before God it will be my heart's delight to worship God and give honour and glory to His Son, the Lord Jesus, for pouring out upon my life streams of His grace in an abundance which turned my hopeless life completely around and gave me a new life full of future and hope.

If you have enjoyed this book and would like to help us to send a copy of it and many other titles to needy pastors in the **Third World**, please write for further information or send your gift to:

**Sovereign World Trust
PO Box 777, Tonbridge
Kent TN11 0ZS
United Kingdom**

or to the **'Sovereign World'** distributor in your country.

If sending money from outside the United Kingdom, please send an International Money Order or Foreign Bank Draft in STERLING, drawn on a **UK** bank to **Sovereign World Trust**.